# NATURE GUIDE
## *to the* NORTHERN FOREST

# NATURE GUIDE
## *to the* NORTHERN FOREST

### EXPLORING THE ECOLOGY OF THE FORESTS OF
### NEW YORK, NEW HAMPSHIRE, VERMONT, AND MAINE

**Peter J. Marchand**

Appalachian Mountain Club Books
Boston, Massachusetts

The AMC is a nonprofit organization and sales of AMC Books fund our mission of protecting the Northeast outdoors. If you appreciate our efforts and would like to make a donation to the AMC, contact us at Appalachian Mountain Club, 5 Joy Street, Boston, MA 02108.

www.outdoors.org/publications/books/

This book was partially funded with a grant from Furthermore, a program of the J. M. Kaplan Fund.

Distributed by The Globe Pequot Press, Guilford, Connecticut.

Front cover photographs: © Jerry and Marcy Monkman,  © Can Stock Photo Inc.,
    ©iStockphoto, ©iStockphoto
Back cover © Jerry and Marcy Monkman
Book design by Cecile Kaufman, X-Height Studio

**Library of Congress Cataloging-in-Publication Data**

Marchand, Peter J.
  Nature guide to the northern forest : exploring the ecology of the forests of New York, New Hampshire, Vermont, and Maine / Peter J. Marchand.
    p. cm.
  Includes index.
  ISBN 978-1-934028-42-1
  1.  Forest ecology--Northeastern States.  I. Title.
  QK117.M37 2010
  581.730974--dc22

                          2010029132

The paper used in this publication meets the minimum requirements of the American National Standard for Information Sciences-Permanence of Paper for Printed Library Materials, ANSI Z39.48-1984. ∞

Interior pages contain 10% post-consumer recycled fiber.
Cover contains 10% post-consumer recycled fiber.
Printed in Canada,
using vegetable-based inks.

**Mixed Sources**
Product group from well-managed forests, controlled sources and recycled wood or fiber
www.fsc.org  Cert no. SW-COC-000952
©1996 Forest Stewardship Council
FSC

10 9 8 7 6 5 4 3 2 1      10 11 12 13 14 15 16 17 18 19 20

*For Mia, Annabelle, and Aidan*

# Contents

Acknowledgments . . . . . . . . . . . . . . . . . . . . . . . . . . . . . . . . . . . . . . . . . ix
Introduction . . . . . . . . . . . . . . . . . . . . . . . . . . . . . . . . . . . . . . . . . . . . . xi

CHAPTER 1

Reading the Landscape:
  The Influence of Nature and Human
  Culture on a Forested Countryside . . . . . . . . . . . . . . . . . . . . . 1
Emergence from an Ice Age . . . . . . . . . . . . . . . . . . . . . . . . . . . . . . . 1
When the North Winds Blow . . . . . . . . . . . . . . . . . . . . . . . . . . . . . . 3
Forest for the Taking . . . . . . . . . . . . . . . . . . . . . . . . . . . . . . . . . . . . . 7
Plant Succession: A Land in Transition . . . . . . . . . . . . . . . . . . . . 13
The Changing Fortunes of Animal Populations . . . . . . . . . . . . . . 18

CHAPTER 2

Plant Communities of the Adirondacks
  and Northern New England . . . . . . . . . . . . . . . . . . . . . . . . . . . 27
Spruce-Fir Woodlands . . . . . . . . . . . . . . . . . . . . . . . . . . . . . . . . . . 28
Heath Bogs . . . . . . . . . . . . . . . . . . . . . . . . . . . . . . . . . . . . . . . . . . . 56
Northern Hardwood Forests . . . . . . . . . . . . . . . . . . . . . . . . . . . . . 68
Subalpine Forests . . . . . . . . . . . . . . . . . . . . . . . . . . . . . . . . . . . . . . 93
Land Above the Trees . . . . . . . . . . . . . . . . . . . . . . . . . . . . . . . . . . 110

CHAPTER 3

Turning Seasons, Turning Cycles . . . . . . . . . . . . . . . . . . . . . . . 131
When a Leaf Falls in the Forest . . . . . . . . . . . . . . . . . . . . . . . . . . 131
Six Months of Winter . . . . . . . . . . . . . . . . . . . . . . . . . . . . . . . . . 143

CHAPTER 4

An Atmosphere of Change . . . . . . . . . . . . . . . . . . . . . . . . . . . . . 153
Climate in Question . . . . . . . . . . . . . . . . . . . . . . . . . . . . . . . . . . 153
Species on the Move . . . . . . . . . . . . . . . . . . . . . . . . . . . . . . . . . . 156

Glossary . . . . . . . . . . . . . . . . . . . . . . . . . . . . . . . . . . . . . . . . . . . . 163
Index . . . . . . . . . . . . . . . . . . . . . . . . . . . . . . . . . . . . . . . . . . . . . . . 167

# Acknowledgments

Many individuals have been involved in the production of this book, some known to me and others not. Heather Stephenson, publisher at AMC, put her confidence in me and gave the green light for this book, while Books Editor Dan Eisner and Production Manager Athena Lakri were charged with pulling the many pieces together and shaping the final product. All three are hardworking and expert at what they do, and to all three I am especially grateful. I extend my gratitude also to Lori Nicholson of Artisan Geographics for her help in producing the map in the introduction of this book and to David W. Fischer at AmericanMushrooms.com for assistance with northern forest fungi. AMC member Sunny Steadman's edits helped improve the readability of this book, and AMC Senior Interpretive Naturalist Nancy Ritger provided valuable feedback. To those I have not mentioned, who labored quietly and competently in the background to see the various aspects of this project through to completion, my sincerest thanks. Without you, this book would be nothing more than an idea.

A grant from Furthermore, a program of the J.M. Kaplan Fund, helped fund production of this book.

# Introduction

When I was a young boy growing up in the Berkshire Hills of Massachusetts, I was enamored with all things natural. I spent countless hours in the fields and woodlots neighboring my home, sometimes to the point of parental concern. I would crawl through the tall grasses in search of interesting insects until my eyes were swollen nearly shut from my allergies. I would slog through marshes in search of frogs and turtles, mindless of leeches attaching themselves to my legs. I collected butterflies, rocks, birds' nests, feathers, and shed snake skins, all of which I carefully curated in the museum of my parents' garage. By the time I was a teenager I could correctly identify almost everything growing in the broadleaf forests of the central Berkshires. Then one summer, on an overnight trip with an Audubon camp group, I was introduced to the spruce-fir forests atop Mount Greylock in northwestern Massachusetts. That little outlier of the northern forest completely captivated me, and it seems my future was determined at that moment. Within a few years I was on my way to the University of New Hampshire, where, in a protracted relationship that lasted a decade and a half, I ended up with a doctorate degree from the botany department, specializing in northern forest ecology.

In the years following my graduate studies I maintained an active research program, first with the Center for Northern Studies and then with Johnson State College, both in northern Vermont, that would lead me ever deeper into the workings of the northern forest. I investigated numerous aspects of spruce swamps, heath bogs, subalpine fir forests, and treeline phenomena. In a cooperative effort with the Appalachian Mountain Club, I studied natural recovery in disturbed alpine tundras, looking for ways to revegetate damaged areas above the treeline. I probed every aspect of these ecosystems including the roles of insects, birds, and mammals. My work was endlessly stimulating and full of learning. I was firmly rooted in the northern forest.

Life, though, is full of unexpected turns and after 44 years in New England I found myself moving to the Sonoran Desert in Arizona and then to the high mountains of Colorado. I feared this was the end of my association with the forests of my earlier years, disqualifying me, as it were, from any further writing about the Northeast. But I was happily wrong. Instead, my work in other ecosystems seems to have sharpened my view and given me a fresh perspective of the northern forest that was my home for so long, allowing me to write about it now with expanded vision. The northern forest, after all, derives its uniqueness only in its relation to other forests of North America.

*Nature Guide to the Northern Forest*, then, is something of a long-term project—an expanded work based on its established predecessor *North Woods*, published by AMC Books in 1987. What I had in mind when I first conceived of *North Woods* was a guide to the workings of northern forests and alpine tundra in the northeastern United States. A number of excellent field guides were available that could assist in the identification of just about anything living, but I wanted to deal more with the *hows* of landscape development and with the functional relationships between organisms and their environment (the truest definition of "ecology"). More than twenty years later, this remains my objective. Of course, executing this ambition turned out to be far more difficult than I imagined, and I ended up with a little of both approaches. In general, I have remained faithful to my initial goals, but it is difficult to talk about bog succession without showing what a few heath shrubs look like, to discuss the distribution of spruces without illustrating the difference between a red spruce and a black spruce, or to talk about habitat associations of animals in the northern forest without putting a few faces to the names. So the reader will find this volume replete with photographs, yet it is by no means intended as a complete field identification manual. In fact, one of the most difficult (and often frustrating) challenges that I have had to accept, for lack of unlimited space, was the need to be selective in the species that I included.

I have written this book primarily with northern New England and the Adirondacks in mind—the region north of a line running roughly from Old Forge, New York, through Rutland, Vermont, to Portland, Maine, and encompassing the High Peaks of the Adirondacks, the northern Green Mountains, and the White Mountains of New Hampshire and Maine. However, the book's usefulness is by no means restricted to this area, for outside of this region lie many pockets of northern hardwood and spruce-fir forest, such as the Mount Monadnock region of southern New Hampshire and Mount Greylock and the surrounding Berkshire Hills in Massachusetts. And of course to our north lies a great expanse of forest in Quebec and the Maritime Provinces for which this book is also appropriate (see accompanying map). Thus, for my purposes I have defined "northern forest" on the basis of vegetation type alone, without reference to political or topographic boundaries. This definition therefore is not the same as the 26 million-acre landscape (spanning northern Maine, New Hampshire, Vermont, and New York), delineated by the Northern Forest Alliance in its "Northern Forest" conservation initiative.

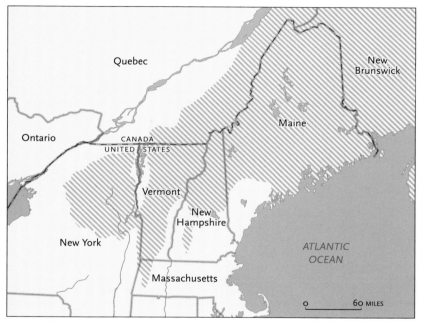

Extent of the northern forest (shaded area) as covered in this book.

Like the geographic area that it covers, this book is something of a mixed bag, a selective odyssey touching on aspects of forest, bog, and alpine ecology that have always interested me and perhaps have caught your own attention. To those of you who share with me a special feeling about these environments, who like nothing better than to hike the mountain trails or canoe the backwaters of the northern forest or maybe just wander around on unpaved roads in an evening, and whose curiosity will never be fully satisfied, I hope this book helps a little.

# Reading the Landscape: The Influence of Nature and Human Culture on a Forested Countryside

## EMERGENCE FROM AN ICE AGE

Just 12,000 years ago, the last great continental ice sheet pulled back from the mountains of northern New England and New York State to reveal a wholly remolded landscape. Gone were the craggy peaks and ridges of the eroding Appalachians; gone were the sharply incised valleys of rivers still cutting their channels downward; and gone, too, were the forests that had previously flourished in the region. The summits were rounded now, worn down by glaciers a mile thick. The river valleys were scoured into wide troughs with smooth, concave sides, as huge tongues of ice had flowed in these natural channels. The soils of the previous millennia were gone, and now the freshly pulverized rock debris strewn about the land was slowly being colonized by a few hardy pioneers of the plant world—a handful of arctic species that survived the Ice Age at the glacier's southern edge. This was the beginning— the preparation of the ground that ultimately would support the Northeast's present forests and alpine tundra.

For perhaps 2,000 years or so, the landscape, covered with tundra vegetation dominated by sedges and dwarf shrubs, resembled the arctic of today. Tundra mammals such as barren ground caribou and musk oxen roamed throughout the area, as evidenced by remains found as far south as the continental shelf area off the Connecticut coast (when much of the earth's water was still tied up in glacial ice, many such shelf areas were dry arctic plains). Gradually, though, the climate warmed; the tundra mammals moved north, following the retreating ice; and boreal forests of spruce and fir appeared on the land. Analysis of pollen grains in pond-bottom sediments and in the peat deposits of bogs shows that spruces were the earliest of the conifers to become established in our area. They first invaded the river valleys and then slowly made their way up the hillsides (see Figure 1), outcompeting the tundra plants for space and resources as they spread. Fir trees soon followed, becoming even more abundant than the spruces, and it wasn't long before firs dominated the higher mountain slopes. As the evergreen forests encroached, the shrinking tundra was gradually pushed higher and higher, finally relegating the last remnants of an arctic landscape to the colder mountain summits and deep ravines, where they persist even today. Meanwhile in the valleys, scattered broadleaf trees were appearing: first the more northern species—aspen, paper birch, and alders—and then, about 9,000 years ago, trees of warmer climates—oaks, ashes, and maples, accompanied by white pine and hemlock. The climate would oscillate a little, becoming warmer than the present for the next 4,000 to 6,000 thousand years, then cooling; and the relative abundance of these species would shrink and swell accordingly. But eventually, a scant 2,000 years ago, the northern hardwoods association dominated by American beech, sugar maple, and yellow birch became established on lower slopes of moderate soil moisture levels throughout the region. And along with the hardwoods, spruce, for some unknown reason, regained prominence on mid-elevation slopes.

**FIGURE 1** The northeastern landscape 10,000 years ago looked much like this scene in interior Alaska. Tundra vegetation dominated most of the region, followed by the slow invasion of spruce-fir forests as the climate warmed.

So time, succession, and the domineering forces of climate all played their part in the greening of this freshly glaciated landscape. Through time, the elements worked to break down old rock into new soil material, releasing nutrients to the young vegetation. The process of succession then brought a series of new plant communities, one after another in steady progression, altering the growing conditions of a site, contributing organic matter to the soil, and recycling nutrients before they were lost downstream. The local climate controlled chemical and biological reaction rates and established limits to the number of species that would compete successfully for the resources of the site. Thus did the Northeast's present forests begin to take shape.

Eventually the European settlers of this region would have an impact on the forests too—something we will discuss in more detail shortly. But long before they arrived, the roots were down, and through all the changes that humans have wrought, the region's woodlands have retained their distinctly northern character, a legacy of glaciers past and climate present.

## WHEN THE NORTH WINDS BLOW

Many factors contribute to the boreal aspect of the northern forest landscape, but none is more important in maintaining this character than the regional climate, for it controls the physical and biological processes that govern the development and organization of plant communities. The climate of this region is, in fact, something of an anomaly; consider, for example, that Old Forge in New York State and Portland, Maine, are situated at the same latitude as the French Riviera but share very few features, climatically or biologically, with the palm-lined Cote d'Azur. Instead, average lowland temperatures in the Adirondack–northern New England region approach those of Anchorage and Helsinki, locations 15 degrees in latitude (almost a thousand miles) farther north. And the weather is still worse in the mountains. Consider that in the White Mountains, treeline barely reaches 4,500 feet above sea level, which makes it one of the lowest anywhere in the world at its latitude (treeline in the northern Rocky Mountains is nearly twice as high). It is often said that the summit of Mount Washington in New Hampshire has the world's worst weather—a subjective judgment certainly, but where hurricane-force winds and subfreezing temperatures can occur in any month of the year, who would argue?

The obvious question, then, is what circumstances create this unusual climatic situation? The answer lies partly in the pattern of atmospheric circulation in the northern hemisphere. Low-pressure systems, whether developing in the tropics or elsewhere, converge on New England like migrating geese on a corn field. In fact, on a map of North American storm tracks (see Figure 2), New England looks like a major freight yard where lines from the South Atlantic, the Gulf region, and even the Pacific Northwest all merge, tending to follow the northern coastline or to move up the St. Lawrence Valley. By itself, this steady progression of transient lows makes for interesting weather changes, but another phenomenon adds to the activity. Because the flow of air around a low-pressure system is counterclockwise, the backside of a low moving out the St. Lawrence Valley or up the coast of Maine always brings with it winds from the north. And these winds are often reinforced by the clockwise circulation of high-pressure cells that develop over the Hudson Bay region. By this circulation pattern, then, every low-pressure system passing over the Northeast tends to drag cold Canadian air in behind it, subjecting the region to frequent intrusions of polar air year-round. This repeating scenario goes a long way toward explaining the Northeast's unusually cool climate.

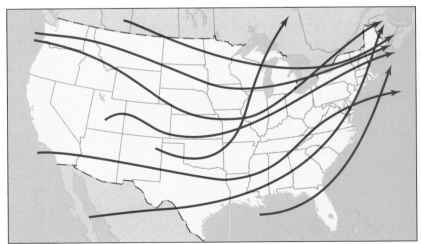

**FIGURE 2** North American storm tracks have a strong tendency to converge over the Northeast. This pattern contributes to the region's relatively cool climate.

An elevational effect that greatly amplifies weather conditions is added to this alternating progression of high- and low-pressure cells. The mountain ranges in the area obstruct the path of moving air, like boulders in a rushing stream, and any air mass swept along in the general circulation of the earth's atmosphere must rise as it encounters these mountain barriers (see Figure 3). As it rises, air expands and cools under the decreasing atmospheric pressure of higher elevations. The air temperature falls an average of 3 degrees Fahrenheit for every 1,000 feet of elevation gain but may drop as much as 5 degrees under cloudless conditions. And when a rising air mass laden with moisture cools below its condensation point (the temperature at which it can no longer hold all the water vapor it contains), cloud cover forms over the mountains, often accompanied by rain or snow showers. It is not surprising, therefore, that the amount of precipitation collected at higher elevations in the Northeast is often double that measured at lowland stations and may reach as much as 80 inches annually. But as impressive as such measurements might be, they still underestimate the amount of moisture available to the high forests. Even when there is no measurable precipitation, the dense needle-leaf canopy of subalpine spruce and fir strains water from every cloud

**FIGURE 3** Air masses cool as they ascend over mountain barriers and often accelerate when squeezed between upper, stable layers of air and the high ridges. This results in greater precipitation and higher wind speeds in the mountains of the Northeast.

that sweeps across the mountain slope, leaving the forest dripping with cool moisture while the rain gauges remain empty.

The net result of this mountain effect is an unusually high frequency of cloud cover over much of the Northeast. The northernmost counties of Vermont and New Hampshire are as cloudy as the Olympic Peninsula in Washington, and this cloudiness, of course, contributes further to the North Country's comparatively low growing-season temperatures.

But the mountain effect doesn't end there. The aspect of a slope (the compass direction it faces) and its exposure to wind also affect the forest microclimate, the climate within and under the canopy of trees. A north-facing slope receives less solar radiation than a south-facing slope and thus tends to be cooler and somewhat wetter, usually supporting more conifers. Likewise, a slope exposed to higher winds will also have a cooler microclimate than it might otherwise. A plant canopy absorbing sunlight usually heats up several degrees if the air around it is calm, but high winds dissipate that heat and thus deny the plants that slight thermal advantage. And when the growing season is short to begin with, slightly reduced temperatures can make a considerable difference in the nature of forest vegetation.

Although it seems to be a contradiction, valley floors in the hill country are cold spots too, but for a very different reason. At night, the ground loses heat through radiational cooling and chills the air, which thus becomes heavier and slowly drains downslope to collect in low areas. On a clear, still night, when radiational cooling is at its greatest, an air-temperature difference of 15 to 20 degrees can develop between a basin and an adjacent hillside just 400 feet or so higher. In such "frost pockets" the growing season is shorter still and the coldest temperatures of winter are recorded.

As a combined result of the atmosphere's general circulation pattern and local topographic effects, only those plant species that are well adapted to cool, short growing seasons and at least occasional winter temperatures of minus 40 degrees or lower are able to proliferate in the northern Appalachians. It is not surprising, then, that much of the natural vegetation of northern New England and the Adirondack region represents a southward extension of Canada's vast boreal forest. Except for the presence of red spruce, whose distribution is largely limited to the northeastern United States, the makeup of our northern forest is much the same as it is throughout southern and central Quebec. Along the meandering stream flats of the colder bottom lands, where the often saturated soils are slow to release their nutrients, only the northern conifers can compete successfully for limited site resources. Often, too, these boreal outliers open up into treeless bogs of acidic peat and heath shrubs—a common sight in the glaciated region of eastern Canada. Elsewhere, on better-drained sites, the northern hardwoods dominate much of the landscape. As we will see shortly, the present expansiveness of hardwood forests in the northern Appalachians may be an artifact of past and present logging practices, but these trees, too, are well adapted to a cool climate, although they generally require better drainage and warmer, richer soils than the lowland conifers. Above 3,000 feet in elevation the northern conifers again dominate the slopes, along with all the associated understory plants of the Canadian boreal forest. And on the highest mountain tops, above treeline, the prostrate shrubs and herbaceous perennials of the alpine tundra take over. These communities, then, make up the northern forest—quiet, enduring, almost mystical forests of gray mists, weathered trees, and sun-flecked, mossy-green floors.

## FOREST FOR THE TAKING

The northern forest might resemble the vast coniferous forests of neighboring Canada even more closely were it not for the lasting influence of early land-use practices following European settlement of New England and the Adirondack region. Our understanding of the landscape before us cannot be complete without some sense of what has happened here in the last 300 years.

When colonists landed in Massachusetts Bay in the early 1600s, they were surprised to find open woodlands with large tracts of land already cleared. This region was home to the Nipmuc, Pokanoket, and Narragansett, whose agricultural practices and never-ending quest for firewood had pushed back the edge of the forests some distance from their settlements. In fact, so consuming was the American Indians' own need for wood that they apparently thought the European settlers had set sail for North America because they had run out of wood back home. (These early impressions have been meticulously researched by Howard S. Russell in *Indian New England Before* the *Mayflower* [University Press of New England, 1980]. The author provides an authoritative review of many original documents and rare notes recorded during initial contact between the Europeans and the Indians of New England.)

The colonists didn't have to venture too far inland, though, to reach old-growth forests of mixed hardwoods and conifers, with trees of a stature probably never before seen by these Europeans. In Massachusetts and southern New Hampshire, they found white pine and hemlock growing 3 feet in diameter and 150 feet tall amid a diverse assemblage of southern broadleaf trees (oaks, hickories, and chestnuts) and the northern hardwoods (beech, maples, and birches). In the mountain regions to the north, however, the colonists found forests of a different character, dominated by spruce and fir that were much more widespread at the time. And growing as they often do—very thickly, with a dense understory of saplings and a tendency to retain stiff, dead lower branches—they must have made progress very difficult for forest explorers; the earliest settlers of New England described forests of the northern Appalachians as "daunting terrible," "full of rocky hills as thick as molehills in a meadow, and clothed with infinite thick woods," "a wrath of savage vegetation."

Conditions changed quickly, however. By the early part of the eighteenth century, settlement of the New York–New England countryside was well under way and forests were falling rapidly to the colonists' bucksaws and axes. Land was being cleared for agricultural purposes, and what had seemed an inexhaustible supply of trees, generally treated as something to be gotten rid of as expediently as possible, was disappearing at an almost unbelievable rate. By the 1830s central New England was as much as 80 percent cleared and, ironically, wood had become so scarce around the major population centers that construction lumber had to be imported by ship from Maine and by rail from areas to the north and west; only the introduction of coal into the cities averted a major fuel crisis. Even in the northern Green Mountains of Vermont, early photographs show the land almost entirely cleared up to elevations of 2,500 feet.

The extension of railroads into northern New England and upstate New York put still more pressure on the area's remaining forests, as low-cost transportation and ready markets to the south spurred new commercial logging ventures. By 1850, lumbering operations had pushed from all directions into the heart of the Adirondack High Peaks region, and less than 30 years later the forest products industry in northern New Hampshire had become one of the leading industries in that state. Pulpwood was in great demand and in many areas clear-cutting was the harvest method of choice. By 1890, almost all conifers of commercial value had been removed from the White Mountains (see Figure 4).

With the disappearance of the forests, the wildlife that once governed the economy of simpler lives vanished too. A number of factors were at work. The large carnivores—wolves, mountain lions, even the black bear—had bounties placed on them almost from the day the Europeans arrived, and extreme hunting pressure contributed to the demise of other game animals. But it was primarily the loss of forest habitat that led to the disappearance

**FIGURE 4** From the beginning of European settlement, timber harvesting has been a force in shaping the northeastern landscape. Forests that re-grew after widespread land-clearing through the late nineteenth century were often different in character from the previous forests.

of so many species, and the list of victims was a long and often surprising one. In 1853, the prominent natural historian Zadock Thompson wrote in his *Natural History of Vermont* of the last known account, twelve years earlier, of a beaver in the state. And although it is hard to believe today, the white-tailed deer and wild turkey, which once sustained so many American Indians, were driven to extinction in these parts too; they were reintroduced by game managers only with the return of suitable forest habitat in the early twentieth century.

What followed this episode of land clearing is an interesting chapter in the forest history of the Northeast and has a direct impact on what we see today. By 1850, the productivity of the northern hill farms had diminished considerably and many residents had second thoughts about farming. The industrial revolution was gaining momentum and promising a better life in the cities, the railroads had opened the rich prairies of the Midwest, and word of gold in California had spread. The lure of all this was great indeed—and then came the Civil War to pull still more young men away from the farm. Agriculture in the north country had seen its brightest days; by the 1860s, farms throughout the region were being abandoned on an unheard-of scale, and the pastures and croplands were simply left to revert back to forestland.

But the same mix of evergreen and broadleaf trees that we see today did not immediately reclaim the fallow land. In the warmer river valleys and lake basins, and in more southern parts, white pine was emerging as never before. The few old pines left scattered throughout the region had provided ample seed that, with its large store of energy, established itself amid the highly competitive pasture grasses. In the colder hill country, the farmlands were often reclaimed by the northern conifers—red and white spruce, balsam fir, and white cedar—which encroached more slowly than the fast-growing white pine, but with equal competitiveness. In these abandoned fields, where grass roots stubbornly held their ground, the conifer seeds seemed to have the edge over the lighter, less drought-resistant seeds of the broadleaf trees.

Where white pine became established, the even-aged stands grew quickly, but because they could not reproduce in their own shade, the pines soon gave the understory over to the more shade-tolerant northern hard-woods. And in just 50 years, the white pines were ready for harvest—a gift of nature to landowners who had invested only taxes on the abandoned acres. By the turn of the twentieth century, a new wave of clear-cutting had begun and another lumber boom was under way throughout the North-east. From 1895 to 1925, an estimated 15 billion board feet of lumber, with a market value of $400 million, was logged off the central New England uplands alone.

In just three decades, the white pine boom was over. The land once more was left to recover on its own, only this time things were different. Instead of being covered with dense pasture grasses, the ground had been thoroughly scarified—the organic floor torn up by the skidding of logs and mineral soil exposed everywhere. And the hardwoods that had earlier established themselves under the pine overstory, and had been ignored by the loggers, were now heirs-apparent to the cleared sites. Before long, their countless progeny sprang up from the bare mineral seedbeds. The face of the land was changing again; by 1930, northern hardwoods dominated throughout much of the region.

By the accounts of early foresters in the northern Appalachians, similar events had been altering the spruce-fir woods. Alfred Chittenden, a forest inspector for the United States Department of Agriculture's Bureau of For-estry, wrote in 1905 that the forests of northern New Hampshire had been "primarily a spruce country but lumbering has brought about a great change in the species." This was echoed some years later by Marinus Westveld, a silviculturist with the United States Forest Service, who wrote that "by 1913 most of the owners in the Northeast were cutting their pulpwood lands clean. . . . Areas which had supported nearly pure stands of spruce and fir were left practically treeless. Elsewhere the hardwoods, not being generally utilized, dominated the residual stand and produced yearly vast quantities of seed, resulting in a greatly increased representation in the following crop." Today, in much of the northern Appalachians, we are looking at that following crop—expansive second-growth forests well suited to the climate and site conditions of the area, but maintained in their present state largely through the discretion of the forest products industry (see Figure 5).

**FIGURE 5** A long history of selective harvesting has altered the composition of forest stands in many areas. Here, all marketable softwoods are being removed, leaving a stand dominated by mixed hardwoods.

# PLANT SUCCESSION: A LAND IN TRANSITION

This brief review of the Northeast's forest history has already introduced the concept of succession and has described several sequences of change in vegetation following disturbance of one sort or another. It is time now to define succession in greater detail, since understanding the northern forest landscape of today requires more than just an appreciation of the land-use history and the way climate influences tree growth. Forests are dynamic, ever changing by their own forces, and the real key to interpreting the present-day distribution of forest communities lies in fully understanding the processes of forest succession.

Succession is the orderly replacement over time of one species or association of species (the community) by another, as a result of competitive interactions between them for limited site resources. Succession occurs because plant species themselves physically modify the site they occupy and do so in a way that shifts the balance of competition from one species to another, making possible the eventual invasion of a site by species that might not have been successful under initial site conditions. Using a simple example, here is how succession might work.

A newly exposed gravel bank, lacking essential nutrients such as nitrogen, is left by a waning glacier or shifting river, and within a short time species A becomes established on it. Species A, a low-growing herbaceous plant, has an advantage because it harbors bacteria in special root nodules that can convert, or fix, atmospheric nitrogen into a form useable by the plant. Other non-nitrogen-fixing plants that arrive at the site find the soil too infertile and soon die out. With each succeeding generation, however, species A contributes organic matter—now containing nitrogen—to the site, slowly increasing the fertility of the soil to the point where species B can successfully invade. Species B—a taller, faster-growing shrub, let's say—soon forms a dense canopy that intercepts much of the light that previously reached the soil surface. Species A, intolerant of shade, gradually disappears, having been outcompeted by species B not for soil nutrients, but for available light. By its own success, species A had changed the site in ways that favor its competitor.

In time, another species (species C) appears, which we'll say is a shade-tolerant conifer. Under the dense shrub cover in the moist organic soil created by the annual litterfall of species B, this newcomer marks time until a local disturbance—perhaps selective cutting by beavers—creates small openings in the shrub canopy. Species C responds to the increased light, grows quickly up through the openings, and eventually forms a new canopy. The acidic nature of decomposing conifer needles now creates soil conditions that render the site less suitable for species B, which gradually disappears. And so the process goes on.

This example represents what is sometimes called floristic relay succession. Not all succession works exactly as illustrated here, but such a model is appropriate for many of the forest communities in our area. As described here, succession ends (or, rather, slows to an imperceptible rate of change until another disturbance occurs) when a species able to reproduce in its own shade attains overstory dominance. This species, or group of species, is likely to be slow-growing, but long-lived—a producer of less abundant but highly successful seed crops and otherwise ideally suited to the particular habitat and able to defend the site from all invaders. The overstory species, along with their associated understory plants, comprise a relatively stable climax community for a given site.

Typically, the role of pioneer—the early colonizer of a new or disturbed site—is played by only a few species that can tolerate the low moisture and nutrients often characterizing a disturbed site. In the northern forest, aspen, gray birch, paper birch, and pin cherry are the most common pioneers among the tree species. These species tend to produce large quantities of seeds yearly—seeds that are adapted for efficient dispersal or long viability in the soil while awaiting an opportunity to germinate. Once established, these trees grow quickly and may completely dominate a site in the early going; but pioneer species are normally short-lived and soon relinquish their ground to others.

These are only generalizations, however, and not all plant succession follows the rules. Whether or not the pioneering tree species in a given situation are hardwoods or conifers often depends on previous land use. We have already seen, for example, that in warmer areas of the northern Appalachian region, white pine is an important pioneer species in abandoned fields. And where white pine does take over, its tenure may be relatively long by virtue of its 300- to 400-year life span. But its place is never permanent. As a closed canopy develops and intercepts more sunlight, the shade-intolerant pine is replaced in the understory by more shade-tolerant species that eventually bring about a change in tree cover. In northern areas, the role of old-field pioneer is sometimes assumed by conifers such as red or white spruce, which we normally think of as late successional species (see Figure 6). When this occurs, much of the usual species progression is short-circuited and the initial community remains stable over time—essentially a climax community right from the start.

**FIGURE 6** Colonization of this abandoned pasture land by pioneering hardwoods is well under way, but the early establishment of conifers here may sidestep the usual progression of species replacement.

The greater ability of the conifers (as opposed to hardwoods) to invade abandoned pastures and hay fields stems mainly from their production of large, relatively heavy, wind-disseminated seeds, which can work down to the soil surface and provide enough stored energy to develop a seedling large enough to compete successfully with the grasses. The natural drought resistance of these conifers also enables the seedling to withstand surface drying and severe root competition for limited water. But such ecological characteristics do not confer any particular advantage in invasion of sites where the mineral soil has been exposed. Whenever disturbance results in the removal of plants and organic litter, exposing bare mineral soil, the fast-growing, relatively shade intolerant pioneer hardwoods are more likely to become established.

As succession proceeds from the early stages of colonization to the point of canopy closure by long-lived shade-tolerant trees, the internal organization within the forest steadily increases. Initially, only a relatively few plant species occupy the site, as the number of pioneers adapted to disturbed conditions is somewhat limited. With time, though, more and more species enter into the picture: species of narrower occupational specialization that partition space and resources ever more intricately in their bid to coexist. Plants with differing light requirements come to occupy different levels of the understory, while roots of differing architecture explore different levels of the soil. Mosses move into the pockets of deep shade, where they retain moisture better, while lichens move up to find light in the crowns of trees. Saprophytic fungi garner sustenance by processing dead plant material as it accumulates on the ground, while parasitic fungi find it easier to tap the already scant energy reserves of aging trees. And so the resources of the site are divided.

With increasing diversity of plants comes an increase in the numbers of animal species too, and the pathways of energy flow in the forest community become still more complex. Meadow voles and jumping mice may dominate the small grassy openings in the early stages of succession, but as the nature of the forest floor changes over time, so does the faunal competition. Accumulating plant litter and deadfalls provide cover for additional animals of varying occupations. Deer mice harvest the fungi that have become so abundant, and in the decaying duff, spiders explore for small insects and fall prey themselves to the hungry short-tailed shrew. The nocturnal flying squirrels move into the rotted-out branch of the old yellow birch and divide feeding

## Understory Tolerance and Forest Succession

The tolerance of tree seedlings to shade in the forest understory is not a characteristic that lends itself to precise measurement, yet common experience tells us that certain species consistently reproduce successfully beneath an overhead canopy, while others almost never do. Knowledge of how one species fares relative to another in this regard proves extremely useful in understanding the successional status of a forest stand: how it came to be what it is and where it is headed in the future.

### Tolerant

Able to survive in deep shade, the following species characterize the northern forest's self-maintaining climax communities:

| | | |
|---|---|---|
| American beech | Eastern hemlock | Sugar maple |
| Balsam fir | Northern white cedar | Red spruce |
| Black spruce | | |

### Intermediate

Wherever understory light is a little more abundant, the following species are able to compete successfully with the more tolerant species:

| | | |
|---|---|---|
| Red maple | White ash | Yellow birch |
| White spruce | | |

### Intolerant

Fast-growing pioneers, the following species are generally unable to survive in shade but persist in northern Appalachian forests as disturbance creates new openings for them:

| | | |
|---|---|---|
| Bigtooth aspen | Eastern white pine | Pin cherry |
| Balsam poplar | Gray birch | Quaking aspen |
| Black cherry | Paper birch | Tamarack |

---

time with the red squirrels who run the day shift. And presiding over all are the larger carnivores and winged raptors.

Thus the food web grows ever wider as forest succession proceeds. The maturing forest is much more than a random assortment of plants and animals. It has become a complex organization of producers and consumers. And in the late stages of succession the forest reaches a kind of dynamic equilibrium—like the pool in a stream in which the flow of energy and materials into and out of it is constant, yet the pool retains a stable organization and functional integrity. In this equilibrium lies a certain resilience, wherein small disturbances merely shift the flow of energy or nutrients from one pathway to another in the complex web, with little effect on the whole.

Although it is indeed a finely tuned ecosystem, the maturing forest can decline in health with age as nutrients are gradually depleted, sequestered for decades or centuries in the woody tissues of old trees, or leached out of the soil and carried downstream to other environments. In this aging condition, the forest may eventually succumb to widespread outbreaks of insects or to wildfire. Such a fate may be considered beneficial in the long run, for disturbance of this nature releases locked-up nutrients and returns the forest to the young and vigorous. In the end, such recurring disturbance, regulated by the shifting tides of energy within the system, preserves the great diversity of plant and animal species that make us all, knowing or not, so much the richer.

## THE CHANGING FORTUNES OF ANIMAL POPULATIONS

With the decline of agriculture in the Northeast after the middle of the nineteenth century and the dramatic reversal of land use throughout the region, many areas in the Adirondacks and northern New England have reverted in less than 100 years from as little as 20 percent to more than 80 percent forest cover. Along with this changing landscape, the numbers of some native animal species have experienced extreme fluctuations—from abundance to extirpation and back again. Some of the species so prominent in the region's pre-settlement forests have vanished, while others are thriving. And in at least one case, a new species has come on the scene to fill a niche vacated by the disappearance of another.

We have already noted that the large carnivores, such as the wolf and mountain lion, were among the first to suffer from the pressures of expanding colonialism—thanks, in part, to concerted efforts on the part of early inhabitants to rid the countryside of them. That these animals were despised by our colonial ancestors is very clear in their writings, which reveal a deep-seated fear of the animals and in many cases an unfortunate ignorance of the regulatory role they played in forest ecosystems. The mountain lion was considered, in the words of naturalist Zadock Thompson, to be the "most insidious and deadly foe of human kind," and wolves, it seems, were a close second. Of the latter, Thompson wrote in his 1853 *Natural History of Vermont* that "slaughter and destruction seemed their chief delight." He painted a picture of bands of wolves roving like street gangs, deliberately terrorizing neighborhoods and looking for trouble wherever they could find it.

Not surprisingly, the wolf and mountain lion carried heavy prices on their heads. The earliest record of a bounty in the New World goes back to 1630 in the Massachusetts colony, where the reward for killing a wolf was set according to the number of livestock in the settlement protected by the heroic deed. But large carnivores need large territories, and the rapid disappearance of habitat for both predator and prey brought about their demise more effectively than any bounty ever levied. In fact, the white-tailed deer, principal prey species of the wolf and mountain lion, was so decimated during the settling of the Northeast that as early as 1779 it had to be protected by law. Thus, by 1800, wolves, too, had become rare in central New York and New England and, according to most accounts, were completely extirpated from all but the remotest areas by the middle of the nineteenth century. Nonetheless, bounties remained in effect into the early twentieth century, with records showing that the state of Vermont paid $20 on one wolf in 1894 and $36 on three wolves in 1902. In the Adirondack region, too, isolated wolf kills continued into the early 1900s.

The mountain lion also was thought to have been extirpated by 1850, although it held out a little longer in remote areas of the Adirondacks. Several were killed there in the late 1870s and the last recorded sighting of that century was in 1894. The state of Vermont also paid a bounty of $20 on a mountain lion in 1895, and in Maine another was reported to have been shot as late as 1906.

Such, then, was the fortune of the big predators. Without adequate habitat and without sufficient refuge within which a breeding population could be maintained, there could be little hope for these animals. But times have changed. Forest succession has come a long way since the turn of the twentieth century—not back to the forests of pre-settlement days, of course, but approaching a maturity that hasn't been seen for a century or more. It is interesting to speculate whether the northern forest might again support the large carnivores.

The return of the mountain lion, in particular, seems an intriguing possibility. In fact, reports of the big cat in the northern forest region have never entirely ceased. Through the 1930s, isolated accounts of mountain lions were reported in Vermont, New Hampshire, and western Massachusetts. By 1950, rumors of sightings in the northern Green Mountains were increasing significantly. The problem with most of these reports, however, was a frustrating lack of verifiable evidence by sources considered authoritative. Then, in the mid 1990s, a breakthrough came with the first official confirmation of a mountain lion in the Adirondack region. In 1993, a senior investigator for the New York State Police reported watching a mountain lion while deer-hunting. His hunting partner later found a fresh deer carcass, partially fed upon and buried under leaf litter in typical cat fashion. When the police investigator returned to the site two days later with a state wildlife biologist, the carcass was nearly half consumed and buried with even more leaves and twigs. The biologist examined the deer carefully and found puncture wounds on opposite sides of the neck, just behind the ears, accompanied by muscle damage and internal bleeding, but with no other marks on either the neck or throat. The spine was broken just below the head. Taken together, the evidence led the biologist to conclude that the deer was indeed killed by a mountain lion. That seemed to open the door: Over the next ten years, laboratory identification of hair samples and DNA tests would confirm isolated instances of lions in Massachusetts, Maine, Quebec, and New Brunswick.

A healthy skepticism still exists among wildlife biologists and state agencies who suggest mountain lions in the Northeast are escapees or intentional releases from captivity. But the possibility of mountain lions slowly returning does not seem too far-fetched, given the present condition of forests in the northern Appalachians and the abundance of prey species in the area, especially of white-tailed deer. These cats are, after all, extremely wide ranging and secretive animals, not often observed by humans, even within their confirmed range. A mountain lion on the move has been known to cover as much as 35 miles in a single night, so it should not seem incredible that one might at least occasionally wander through some remote corners of northern New England and the Adirondack region. Whether or not they are taking up residence, though, is a matter of continuing debate. The states of Maine, New Hampshire, and New York still consider this species "officially" extirpated, while the Vermont Endangered Species Committee affords the mountain lion legal protection with endangered species status.

There has been much speculation about the possible return of the wolf in northern New England and the Adirondacks, as well, though it has been difficult to determine whether the infrequent sightings have been of truly wild animals or if they have been of illegal pets that may have been bred with domestic dogs such as the malamute. Debate has been stimulated, however, by the shooting, in 2008, of a confirmed eastern gray wolf that had killed several sheep in western Massachusetts, just south of the Vermont border. It would be extraordinary for this animal to have migrated several hundred miles southward from Ontario (the closest established population of the gray wolf today), but not impossible given the nature of the animal. The larger question, though, is whether or not the gray wolf would still find an ecological role in our northern forest, since its long vacated niche as a predator seems to have been assumed by a well-established newcomer, the eastern coyote.

The eastern coyote was first sighted in Vermont and New Hampshire in the early 1940s and has since spread throughout New England and upstate New York. Widely labeled a "coydog"—a hypothetical cross between a coyote or fox and a domestic dog—the eastern coyote, when it initially showed up, soon proved to be a new species, the outcome of crossbreeding between a northern subspecies of western coyote and the Ontario wolf (the eastern coyote is significantly larger than the western coyote), followed by a slow eastward migration and adaptation to a new environment. In essence, the eastern coyote was a sort of new wolf, a slightly smaller and more opportunistic animal better adjusted to human activities and the more fragmented forests of the twentieth century—a new predator that had arrived to fill a vacant niche in a landscape that had been without a large predator for a while (see Figure 7). And its lifestyle is apparently well suited to the Northeast's current countryside, for the coyote is enjoying considerable success, with numbers estimated in the thousands throughout the northern Appalachians. The eastern coyote is a significant new contribution of the twentieth century, a product of landscape evolution as much as animal evolution, and it looks like it is here to stay, at least as long as our forests remain in their present condition.

**FIGURE 7** The eastern coyote is a latecomer to the northern forest. Biologists believe this subspecies evolved from crossbreeding between the western coyote and the Ontario wolf as the smaller western coyote slowly expanded its range eastward.

One animal that is unlikely to stage a comeback in the northern forest is the woodland caribou. The woodland caribou is a habitat specialist, dependent upon expansive old-growth conifer forests and peatlands, where it relies upon an abundance of arboreal and ground lichens for sustenance. And clearly, old-growth forests—long vanished from the region except for a few isolated forest stands—are not something that can be re-created at will. So the woodland caribou in northeastern North America, in the face of shrinking habitat, has become confined to Newfoundland, Labrador, and northern Quebec, having been completely displaced from the Canadian Maritime Provinces and northern Maine where it once thrived.

Apart from a scarcity of old-growth forest, a significant roadblock in the caribou's return may be the greatly increased numbers of white-tailed deer in the Northeast. Repeated attempts at reintroducing the woodland caribou to Maine's largest protected area, Baxter State Park (where, ostensibly, the last native caribou in Maine was sighted in 1908), have ended in failure, blamed partly on predation of caribou calves by bears, but also on interaction between the caribou and white-tailed deer. Unlike the caribou, white-tailed deer thrive in a patchwork landscape of early successional forests and clearings, such as are perpetuated by the many small-scale logging and farming activities in the North Country. An abundance of ideal habitat in early twentieth century New England and upstate New York, coupled with the absence of large predators, led to an explosion in the number of deer, pushing them, some believe, deeper into unbroken conifer forests where they likely came into contact with the caribou. Simple competitive interaction was not the effect of this contact, however, with one species eventually outdoing and excluding the other. The interaction involved a third party, a brain parasite carried by the deer. The brainworm, actually a roundworm or nematode, is normally non-debilitating to its white-tailed host, but has proven fatal when transferred to the caribou. Contact between the white-tailed deer and caribou, with subsequent transfer of the parasite, is thought to have dealt the final blow to the caribou of New Brunswick and Nova Scotia. An effort in the late 1960s to reintroduce caribou into Nova Scotia failed after a herd of 51 transplants apparently fell victim to the brainworm.

The story of the wild turkey also serves to illustrate the changing fortunes of animal populations with landscape succession in the northern forest region. It was once so plentiful that it was the very symbol of bounty in the New World. But like so many other game animals native to the area, the turkey had disappeared from the Northeast by the middle of the 1800s. Certainly early New Englanders' insatiable appetite for this great bird contributed to its demise, but even without such hunting pressure it could not have survived the forest changes that have occurred over the last 200 years.

The wild turkey (see Figure 8) is a bird of mature hardwood forests, not of corn fields, or hedgerows, or small disjunct woodlots. It had no place in the agricultural boom of the early 1800s, nor even in the farm-abandonment era of the late 1800s, for neither its feeding preferences nor its survival skills lend themselves to early successional forests. The turkey survives by scratching in the leaf litter for mast, and it depends on sharp eyesight in an open understory for evasion of predators. It is also something of an opportunist, digging for tuberous roots (starch storage organs like potatoes), eating fruits and

**FIGURE 8** Wild turkeys have prospered as northern hardwood forests have matured in the last century. The large nut of the beech tree is a staple in their diet.

seeds from a number of plants, and even picking up insects and slugs when it finds them. The turkey depends heavily on the large seeds of the climax hardwood trees—acorns and hickory nuts in its southern range and beech nuts in the northern forest. When the mast crop is good, winter survival is noticeably better and reproduction swings upward. When the crop is poor, the turkey suffers.

During difficult winters when the snow is deep and the mast crop has been poor, the turkey may derive some benefit by picking up seeds from the manure that northern hill farmers spread out over the snow (one game biologist has referred to this as a hot-lunch program for turkeys). But this bird's success today, following reintroduction in the middle of the twentieth century, depends little on the helping hand of humankind. The story of the turkey's comeback is a story of landscape succession, and if we have influenced the process, it has been through decades of cutting practice that has maintained the northern hardwoods as we now know them. The distribution of the wild turkey in the northern Appalachians today exceeds its precolonial range probably because the distribution of hardwood forest in the north exceeds its precolonial range; and this maturing forest is abundant with beech, thanks in part to selective cutting practices and a poor market for the wood of this tree.

As the wild turkey prospers in our maturing hardwood forests, another familiar bird, the ruffed grouse, is not faring so well, for the ruffed grouse is something of an early successional counterpart to the turkey. Like the turkey, the overwinter success of the grouse depends heavily on a single preferred food source—in this case, the buds of the pioneering quaking aspen. The grouse will feed on the buds of other tree species too, but aspen offers two distinct advantages: the buds, particularly of male flowers, are an exceptionally high energy source, and the branches on which they are clustered are stout and easy to feed from. This enables the feeding grouse to fill its crop quickly while minimizing its exposure to predators, particularly owls. (In the winter the grouse spends about fifteen minutes each evening, just before sundown, frantically filling its crop, and then dives into the snow where it spends the night digesting this energy.) In our mature forests yellow birch is often the grouse's species of choice, but these trees have only small clusters of buds or catkins at the ends of flimsy branches, requiring much fluttering and commotion for food of comparatively low nutritive value. So the ruffed grouse is as dependent on early successional aspen groves as the turkey is on later successional forests. Regardless of whatever else is available, studies have shown that where there is no aspen in the forest canopy, grouse rarely overwinter successfully and breeding birds are seldom found. And aspen, being a short-lived pioneer species, is now dwindling in numbers as the forests that reclaimed the twentieth century landscape pass into maturity and give way to the climax tree species.

# CHAPTER 2

# Plant Communities of the Adirondacks and Northern New England

At first glance, the complex mosaic of vegetation covering the hillsides and valleys of the northern Appalachian region may appear no more orderly than the splotches of color on an artist's palette. But if we look closely, with an eye sensitive to subtle changes in shade and texture, we soon find that we can discriminate between different plant community types—the mottled greens of mixed hardwoods, the lighter shades of aspen groves, the soft lacy texture of tamarack stands—and we begin to see patterns in the landscape that are not at all random. As we attempt to sort out these patterns, we find it possible to divide the landscape into a number of more or less discrete units, not unlike those of a jigsaw puzzle, but with an added dimension or two. The pieces of this puzzle are the plant communities themselves, associations of plant species that we recognize as belonging together under certain circumstances. In this puzzle, the pieces are put together according to topographic position; that is, the puzzle is assembled on a three-dimensional surface and each piece has its proper place depending on its particular site requirements. A lowland cedar community will not fit on a dry hillside, and a hillside beech-maple community will not coexist with fir on a high summit. But neither will the beech-maple community fit on a hillside dominated by an aspen-birch community, because the two represent different successional stages; that is, one normally precedes the other on a given site. So we have the added dimension of time in this puzzle.

Once we have the pieces of the puzzle sorted out—once we understand the basics of forest succession and how climate and local topography affect the distribution of vegetation types—then it becomes relatively easy to fit all the pieces together and to read into the landscape a great deal about its past history and present condition. Let's look now at the basic units of this puzzle and see how these communities are made up, how they function ecologically, and how they combine to form an integrated landscape.

## SPRUCE-FIR WOODLANDS

Spruce and fir dominate the forests of cold hollows, meandering stream flats, and higher mountain slopes throughout the northern Appalachians. These conifers, superbly adapted to temperature and nutrient limitations of northern regions, are able to prosper under growing conditions that exclude most other tree species. Sites supporting spruce-fir forests are generally nutrient-poor, either because they receive very little nutrient input to begin with, as in the case of high-elevation forests, or because they are so cold that decomposer organisms responsible for the breakdown of organic matter are relatively ineffective. In addition, the acidification of these soils by the conifer litter itself, which is very low in base ions, compounds the problem because some nutrients, like phosphorous, become insoluble under acid conditions and thus cannot be absorbed.

Conifers have a considerable advantage on these sites. They conserve nutrients because they do not have to produce all new foliage every year (tamarack being the exception), and the evergreen habit of these species extends their photosynthetic season beyond that of deciduous trees, particularly in the spring of the year (see "The Evergreen Advantage" on page 42). Furthermore, these trees can withstand winter temperatures of minus 80 degrees and colder without injury.

The different conifers that dominate our spruce-fir woodlands show fairly distinct site preferences, tending to segregate themselves along the slope from bottom land to treeline. Species that are sometimes confusing to identify, like red spruce and black spruce, can often be distinguished by the habitat where they are found. It is convenient, then, to discuss these trees and the communities they form in the order in which they occur along the slope—just as we might encounter them while hiking up a mountain trail.

Black spruce and balsam fir are the species of extremes and are found at both ends of the slope. In the poorly drained flats of the northern lowlands, black spruce is usually abundant but may share dominance with balsam fir and others tolerant of wet soils, especially tamarack. Together these species comprise the lowland conifer swamps, perhaps the most diverse of the spruce-fir community types. In this habitat the trees are rooted in a spongy organic soil that may be flooded part of the year, providing only a very shallow aerated zone for root activity. As a result, growth rates are slow and understory regeneration limited. Black spruce often has the advantage in these moist environments, in that it reproduces quite readily by vegetative means, as well as by seed. As lower branches come into contact with the mossy ground surface, roots develop from stem tissue no longer exposed to the air and sunlight. The branches then turn upright to become self-sustaining trees. Few other species can establish themselves under such swampy conditions, and even fir and larch may require a rotting log or stump to get started, because the ground often is too wet or acidic for successful seedling establishment.

With the constraints imposed by cold, saturated soils, lowland spruce-fir forests tend to be less dense than high-elevation forests. As a result, ample light reaches the forest floor and supports the growth of many understory shrubs and herbaceous plants that give this forest community a richness of species lacking in the subalpine spruce-fir zone (discussed shortly). Some of the more conspicuous shrubs of these lowlands are Labrador tea, low sweet blueberry and velvet-leaved blueberry, winterberry, black chokeberry, sheep laurel, and mountain holly. Among the herbaceous plants are a number of northern species such as Canada mayflower, bunchberry, creeping snowberry, starflower, clintonia, goldthread, twinflower, and wood sorrel. In older stands where sufficient light reaches the inner branches of the canopy, the trees themselves often become draped with lichens (see "Lichens" on page 120), most notably the old man's beard that recalls the Spanish moss draping the graceful oaks of the deep South (Spanish "moss," though, is neither a moss nor a lichen, but is actually a flowering vascular plant). In the Canadian boreal forest these lichens are an important source of food for foraging caribou in winter.

It should be noted in passing that white cedar, too, often occurs in wet areas, occasionally in pure stands (cedar swamps), but almost always along stream or pond margins where there is some circulation of groundwater. Cedar is less tolerant of the acidic conditions and low nutrient levels normally associated with the development of spruce-fir swamps.

On better-drained sites, black spruce does not compete successfully with other species and is completely replaced by red or white spruce. In the northern border sections of Vermont, New Hampshire, and Maine, wherever soils are deep and well drained, white spruce often dominates. This species increases in abundance northward into the Canadian boreal forest but curiously does not extend its range into the subalpine forests of the northern Appalachians as do the many other boreal species that find a niche here. A few scattered individuals of white spruce have been found on the north side of Camel's Hump in Vermont, but there is reason to suspect that these were introduced.

Thus, on the middle slopes, red spruce is the most abundant conifer. It usually mixes with hemlock and hardwoods, but occasionally, where soils are poor, it is found in pure stands. Red spruce increases in number with elevation and generally becomes the dominant forest species in the lower reaches of the subalpine spruce-fir zone, at elevations around 3,000 feet. Continuing upward, however, the relative abundance of red spruce and balsam fir shifts, and fir becomes dominant at elevations above 3,500 feet. Thus we can distinguish a lower-elevation "spruce phase" and an upper-elevation "fir phase" in our subalpine forests. Red spruce may be found right up to treeline, but at the upper limit of tree growth in the northern mountains, black spruce reappears and together with balsam fir forms the krummholz, the zone of gnarled and matted growth at treeline.

It would be misleading to leave the impression here that spruce-fir woodlands consist of conifers only. In fact, hardwoods may comprise a minor part of the forest canopy almost anywhere. Paper birch, for example, is widely scattered throughout the range of spruce-fir habitats right up to the treeline. The wetter sites at low elevations may also host scattered red maples, and along the riverbanks balsam poplar is often common. (Balsam poplar is the tree that flutters in the breeze and looks much like aspen, but has triangular leaves and a balsam fragrance.) On better-drained sites, quaking aspen often invades small openings. At higher elevations, mountain maple and mountain ash are common amid the conifers, as are shrubs like hobblebush, wild raisin, and mountain serviceberry.

**EASTERN HEMLOCK**
*(Tsuga canadensis)* Crown
thin and lacy-textured,
terminal leader and branch
tips often drooping at
ends. Cones elliptical, less
than .75 inches long, hanging at ends of twigs. Bark
medium to dark brown
in color, scaly in young
trees but becoming deeply
furrowed with age. Once a
commercial source of tan-
nin for leather processing.

**EASTERN WHITE PINE**
*(Pinus strobus)* Top branches arched strongly upward. Bark smooth greenish-grey on younger trees, becoming cracked and furrowed with age. Needles attached in bundles of five; cones 5 to 8 inches long. Tall, straight trunks were reserved for ship masts in colonial times.

**BALSAM FIR *(Abies balsamea)*** Foliage predominantly blue-green in color with tree crowns compact, tapering to a sharp "spire." Cones grow upright near the top of the tree. Bark in younger trees relatively smooth with prominent pitch blisters that break easily when pressed. Harvested primarily for pulpwood.

**BLACK SPRUCE (*Picea mariana*)** A somewhat stunted tree usually growing in saturated soils. Foliage dark blue-green to olive-green with crowns scraggly and lateral branches short. Bark thin, gray-brown, and scaly. Needles .5 inches long or less, with numerous hairs on new growth. Small cones remain on tree for several years.

**RED SPRUCE (Picea rubens)** Branches stiff and spreading, giving crown a more rounded conical form. Foliage yellowish- to olive-green with needles .5 to .75 inches long. Cones less than 1.5 inches long. Bark is dark and coarse. Exudes sticky, yellowish resin deposits gathered commercially in the nineteenth century for chewing gum.

**TAMARACK *(Larix laricina)*** A tree mostly of wet, organic soils. Crown has somewhat wispy appearance imparted by long and flimsy branches. Needles are clustered, turning pale gold and dropping in autumn. Fine roots were used by Chippewa to sew birch bark strips together for canoes.

**NORTHERN WHITE CEDAR *(Thuja occidentalis)*** Found mostly in wet areas with neutral to alkaline soils. Evergreen leaves are small and flattened in overlapping scales. Bark peels in long, thin strips. Foliage high in vitamin C and thought to be the source of tea that cured explorer Jacques Cartier's party of scurvy in 1595–96.

**CREEPING SNOWBERRY (Gaultheria hispidula)** Low, trailing evergreen. Produces small white berries with the taste of wintergreen; sometimes made into preserves. Leaves can also be used for a mild tea. A common host plant for caterpillars of the bog fritillary butterfly.

**GOLDTHREAD (Coptis trifolia)** Member of the buttercup family. Name derived from bright golden-yellow runners connecting plants below ground. Root used for dye; also dried and brewed as a tea for treatment of mouth cankers. Leaves shiny, evergreen.

**CANADA MAYFLOWER (Maianthemum canadense)** Botanical name means "May blooming." An unusual member of the lily family, having four petals and stamens, instead of the usual three-parted symmetry. Stalk zigzagged with leaf bases wrapping around the stem. Flowers produce red berries in autumn; favored by spruce grouse.

**BUNCHBERRY *(Cornus canadensis)***
Herbaceous member of the dogwood family. Large white "petals" are actually bracts surrounding small greenish flowers. Gives rise to a cluster of bright red berries, which are edible, but not very tasty. A mild tea from its roots has been used to treat cholic.

**CLINTONIA *(Clintonia borealis)*** Named for former governor of New York and avid botanist DeWitt Clinton, who served in the early nineteenth century. Unusual in having true-blue fruit, giving the plant its other name, "blue bead lily." Young leaves are edible; crushed leaves rubbed on skin are said to repel mosquitoes.

**STARFLOWER *(Trientalis borealis)***
Distinguished by its unique combination of seven-petaled flowers rising above a single whorl of shiny, lance-shaped leaves. Genus name translates to "one-third of a foot," referring to the average height of the plant. A member of the primrose family.

**TWINFLOWER *(Linnaea borealis)*** Low, trailing, evergreen plant with paired, nodding flowers having a fragrance similar to honeysuckle. Circumpolar in distribution; named for Carolus Linnaeus, the father of modern botany, by Linnaeus's teacher and adopted as the official emblem of Linnaeus's home province in Sweden.

**WOOD SORREL *(Oxalis montana)*** Flower petals white, strongly veined in pink. Leaves heart-shaped, clover-like, folded in the middle. Leaves close at night or in the rain. All parts have strong acidic or sour flavor imparted by presence of oxalic acid.

**ARETHUSA *(Arethusa bulbosa)*** A striking orchid primarily of sphagnum bogs. Grows from a perennial tuber that may not produce a flower every year, thus appearing to fluctuate in number from year to year. Named for the mythical Greek nymph, daughter of Nereus.

An important aspect in the ecology of spruce-fir forests wherever they are found is repeated natural disturbance in one form or another. Wind throw is the most common disruptive force in the mature forest stand, owing to the shallow rooting of both red spruce and balsam fir. Breakage under heavy snow load may also occur at high elevations, especially with balsam fir, which does not produce as strong a wood as spruce and which also becomes susceptible to decay as it weakens in old age (being 70 to 80 years in this species). As a result of this kind of disturbance, mature spruce-fir stands are often characterized by numerous small openings in the canopy.

The effects of disturbance on this vegetation can be varied, and depend not only on the nature and extent of the disturbance but also on the presence or absence of tree seedlings in the understory prior to disturbance. In some cases recurring disturbance contributes to the continual rejuvenation of the climax community. Because both red spruce and balsam fir are very shade tolerant and can maintain themselves for a long time under a closed canopy, the normal response to a sudden opening is a growth spurt in understory trees. It is not at all unusual to see these two species dominating such openings to the complete exclusion of all others. As long as there is adequate reproduction in the understory, disturbance on this scale (which might also include the selective cutting of trees) will maintain an equilibrium in the community, where mortality and reproduction are in continual balance. This process can slowly alter species composition, however, as sudden openings almost always favor the more prolific and faster-growing balsam fir.

Where site conditions are well suited for the conifers and where reproduction by these species under the canopy is adequate, the spruce-fir community may be quite stable and resistant to change. In the absence of understory regeneration, however, any disturbance to this community may bring about a major shift in vegetation type. On better-drained sites an opening of the canopy, especially if accompanied by scarification of the soil, may result in the rapid influx of shade-intolerant and fast-growing hardwoods, principally paper birch, yellow birch, pin cherry, and mountain maple. Lacking competition from conifer reproduction, these hardwoods grow vigorously and may occupy the site for a considerable length of time; the period depends primarily on the condition of the substrate. If the soil is deep and well drained, the later seeding of shade-tolerant sugar maple and beech could eventually bring about a long-term change in cover type, a change that we have witnessed in many

## The Evergreen Advantage

IT IS COMMONLY thought that the advantage of evergreen leaves lies in their ability to photosynthesize year round. While this may be the case for evergreens in milder winter climates, available evidence indicates that it is not so for conifers in the northern forest. Photosynthesis in these trees appears to stop with the cessation of active growth and the onset of cold acclimation, the active process of acquiring tolerance to freezing in the fall. Throughout most of the winter, the chloroplasts (the site of photosynthesis) in the conifer needle are found clumped together in an inactive state and remain devoid of any starch grains that would indicate photosynthetic activity. And no evidence suggests that the photosynthetic apparatus is able to reorganize itself and start up during brief periods of midwinter thaw. However, as early as mid-March starch begins to accumulate in the needles again, indicating that photosynthesis has resumed. Thus our conifers have the advantage of being able to start up early and to extend the usual photosynthetic season by six or eight weeks.

The primary advantage of the evergreen leaf, though, may be related to nutrient conservation. To understand how this works, let's think about plant growth in economic terms. Imagine that a living plant operates under the same constraints as a manufacturing business, where operating capital is invested in new machinery with the expectation of realizing a reasonable return on the investment. If working capital is in short supply, this machinery may have to be kept in service longer to maximize the investment return, even if the machinery becomes less efficient with age. The hard reality is that only those with surplus capital can afford to reinvest regularly in new machinery.

In green plants, part of the investment capital used to construct photosynthetic machinery comes from the soil nutrient bank. This machinery (the leaves) then uses atmospheric carbon dioxide and sunlight to provide high-energy carbohydrates that make possible additional growth in other parts of the plant. It takes nutrients, then, to build leaves, and if nutrients are in short supply, the evergreen leaf is a better investment for the simple reason that it lasts longer. The evergreen leaf is not quite as efficient photosynthetically, but it yields a return over a period of years and thus gives back more for the amount of nutrients invested. It is no coincidence that evergreens are commonly found growing in nutrient-deficient environments, for the evergreen conserves nutrients, and that may be its greatest advantage.

---

logged-over areas throughout northern New England and the Adirondacks. If the site is of poorer quality, the stand of successional hardwoods may be only temporary, with conifers eventually reassuming dominance.

While optimal site conditions for plant species are often narrowly defined, as plants have to compete successfully for their needs while rooted in place, few mammals of the northern forest are restricted entirely to one community or another. This is not to suggest that mammals do not prefer certain types of habitats, but rather that mammals are mobile and are sometimes displaced by exclusion from others' territories into peripheral habitat where they survive, but may not reproduce successfully.

Of some 40 species of mammal commonly found in our northern forest, perhaps the northern water shrew has the most restrictive distribution, being dependent almost entirely upon dense, grassy vegetation along water courses, primarily in the spruce-fir woodlands. So tied to water is this small mammal that it has become partially adapted to an aquatic life. The toes on its hind feet are webbed at the base and fringed with stiff hairs to aid in swimming as it forages underwater for aquatic insects. The water shrew is not, of course, the only mammal of our spruce-fir woodlands that is dependent on aquatic or riparian habitats. Mink and river otter are equally at home here (where both may prey upon the water shrew), but, unlike the half-ounce water shrew, mink and otter have large home ranges and in winter, especially, will travel considerable distances overland, through hardwood forests as well as spruce-fir woodlands, to find open water and food.

The red squirrel also shows strong habitat affinity, being heavily dependent upon an adequate supply of conifer seeds for its over-winter success. So important is this source of food to red squirrels, and so aggressive are they in defense of their established territories, that individuals (usually juveniles) pushed to the periphery of good spruce-fir habitat are often at risk, especially during winter, and suffer considerable mortality. Northern flying squirrels are also commonly associated with spruce-fir forests, where lichens and fungi are a staple item in their diets. However, being less restrictive in their feeding habits than red squirrels, they are frequently found in mixed conifer-hardwood forests as well. The marten, an important predator of both squirrel species, is similarly associated with spruce-fir woodlands. Martens, though, prefer continuous, mature forest cover and are quite sensitive to habitat fragmentation. Consequently, their numbers have varied widely with changing land-use patterns in different parts of the Northeast. While marten trapping is still permitted in northern Maine and in the Adirondacks, this species is now listed as threatened in New Hampshire and endangered in Vermont.

The snowshoe hare may well be the most emblematic mammal of our spruce-fir woodlands, along with its quintessential predator (but by no means its only one), the Canadian lynx. The relationship between these two species, with their parallel population fluctuations, is a classic story in the literature of predator-prey interactions. Snowshoe hares throughout North America exhibit prominent peaks and troughs in their numbers over time, with a cycle generally lasting eight to eleven years. Explanations for this phenomenon range from reproductive failure in hares caused by the toxins that plants produce in response to heavy grazing pressure during the peak of the population, to an increase in numbers of predators that starts the downslide in hare numbers and eventually brings about a crash in predator numbers. The cycle starts anew with recovery of hares, as either the plant toxins diminish following the subsequent decline in browsing pressure, or predation pressure relaxes following the crash of predators. (Neither of these hypotheses accounts for a greater mystery, however: Population peaks and troughs appear to be synchronized, over the entire North American range of the snowshoe hare, with cyclic fluctuations in the number of sunspots— temporary areas of reduced temperature—on the surface of the sun. No explanation has yet been offered for this phenomenon.)

In any case, we know that herbivores affect plants and plants affect herbivores, and that predators can, by extension, affect both. Where snowshoe hares are especially abundant, their constant, selective browsing of favored foods can have a decided effect on species composition and succession of the community. The same is true of other prominent herbivores: A classic case study comes from spruce-fir forests on Isle Royale, Michigan (similar in nature to spruce-fir forests in the Northeast), where high numbers of moose have long suppressed the growth of balsam fir through heavy browsing. When wolves reached the island in 1950 (by crossing an ice bridge between the island and mainland), moose populations began to decline and balsam fir recovered. Thus the predator had an effect on plant succession.

The Canadian lynx could similarly temper the effects of snowshoe hare browsing in our region, except for one major hitch: The lynx here has fallen onto hard times in spite of an abundance of its favored prey species. And

## Spruce Budworm

SPRUCE BUDWORM can be a major disturbance factor in our spruce-fir woodlands, but its name is a half-truth. The "worm" is actually a caterpillar, an insect larva complete with three pairs of legs. (Worms lack legs and are in a different phylum altogether.) This caterpillar is the progeny of a small, mottled, brown and gray moth that mimics the bark of the tree or a patch of lichen in appearance. And while any of the spruces can serve as host to this insect, balsam fir is actually its preferred food source (the range of the eastern spruce budworm closely matches the range of balsam fir) and it is this tree that suffers the most damage from spruce budworm outbreaks. There is no half-truth, however, about this small caterpillar's appetite for the buds and needles of its favorite tree species.

Outbreaks of the spruce budworm are cyclic, severe, and extensive, both in area and in duration. Researchers at the University of Quebec have used sophisticated tree-ring analysis to reconstruct the history of spruce budworm outbreaks in the Gaspé region just above the tip of Maine, identifying eleven outbreaks in the region between 1577 and 2004. The average duration of the budworm outbreaks was 14 years and the average time from the midpoint of one outbreak to the midpoint of the next was 40 years, until the twentieth century when the time interval shortened to 33 years. A strong synchrony between the dates and duration of outbreaks identified in the Gaspé region and those reported by other researchers in eastern and central Quebec suggests that spruce budworm outbreaks are also extensive in nature, affecting entire regions.

Spruce budworm outbreaks run their course when defoliation has proceeded to the point of insect starvation, or when natural predators, parasites, and disease begin to decrease insect numbers. Conditions leading to an outbreak are harder to pinpoint, but likely have to do with the gradually declining vigor of host trees as they age, following regeneration after the last outbreak. While the extensive defoliation caused by spruce budworm is destructive in an economic and aesthetic sense, the insect is, after all, native to our region—a natural part of our northern forest ecosystem—and its ups and downs over the centuries undoubtedly have had much to do with the shaping of our spruce-fir woodlands.

the probable cause for its decline—habitat fragmentation—is beginning to sound familiar. Our region lies at the southern range limit of the Canadian lynx, and continuity of habitat between northern New England and Quebec is thought to have played an important role in the presence of the lynx here. The lynx, though, like the marten, is an animal preferring uninterrupted wilderness areas. Habitat fragmentation, perhaps especially the development of agriculture in the Saint Lawrence plains of southern Quebec, is apparently impairing the Canadian lynx's ability to disperse southward from population centers in the Canadian provinces. So it now faces a most difficult situation in our northern forest: isolation combined with critically low numbers. Nonetheless, a small resident population in northern Maine and occasional sightings elsewhere keep it on the list of iconic mammals of our spruce-fir woodlands.

Birds, as well as mammals, show strong affinities with particular plant communities, and the number of species associated with the northern forest is impressive. The majority, some 100 species or so, are migratory birds that arrive in the region in April or May to breed, and four months later begin their journey southward again to spend winter in the warmer climate of the lower latitudes. The black-throated green warbler, Swainson's thrush, and blackburnian warbler are among the more familiar birds that breed in our spruce-fir woodlands and winter as far south as Venezuela. Other familiar migrants, like the white-throated sparrow, yellow-rumped warbler, and golden-crowned kinglet, may move only relatively short distances, spending winter in coastal areas from southern New England southward to Florida. And many of these migrants are extraordinarily faithful to a particular area, even a particular nest site when they return to the northern forest. It seems almost incomprehensible that a small bird can make the round-trip from northern New England or upstate New York to the tropics and beyond, and return to the same tree at the end of its journey, yet this has been recorded for both the northern parula, breeding in low-elevation spruce-fir woodlands, and the blackpoll warbler of higher subalpine forests.

Most of these migrants are insect-eaters (though typical seed-eaters can become insectivorous when rearing young), and they find food resources abundant and concentrated during the relatively short breeding season. Some are even linked to the cycles of the northern forest's major forest defoliators. The population density and reproductive success of at least two species common to spruce-fir woodlands, the Cape May warbler and the bay-breasted warbler, appear to be positively correlated with the abundance of spruce budworm. It is the specialized feeding habits of these summer residents, however, that require them to leave at the end of the season. The flycatchers, for example, are so specialized at catching insects on the wing that they have no options when insects are no longer flying. Foliage-gleaning warblers are out of luck when the myriad caterpillars of summer have metamorphosed into adulthood, laid their eggs, and died. The ground-feeding thrushes have no alternative but to go south when insects are inactive and the land is covered with snow.

Thus, winter in the northern forest belongs to birds whose morphological or behavioral adaptations, perhaps much more than their cold tolerance, enable them to survive during the dormant season. These are primarily of two groups: the bark gleaners—birds like woodpeckers, nuthatches, creepers, and chickadees that scour the crevices of trees for dormant insects—and seed-eaters, particularly those specialized at dismembering the cones of spruce and fir. Of the bark gleaners, the three-toed and black-backed woodpeckers, boreal chickadee, and red-breasted nuthatch are most closely associated with spruce-fir woodlands; and of the seed eaters, pine and evening grosbeaks, white-winged and red crossbills, and pine siskins are the most common. There are others too, of course. The opportunistic gray jay and northern raven are easily among the most familiar, and successful, of the area's winter birds. But if there is one species that is inextricably tied to our coniferous forests, it is the spruce grouse.

The spruce grouse lives in conifer forests across all of Canada and Alaska, reaching its southernmost limit in northern New England and the Adirondacks. Superbly adapted to this forest type, the bird specializes in feeding on the foliage of spruce and fir. While it will pick at insects and berries in summer (heath shrubs are an important component of its preferred habitat), as well as mushrooms and tender herbaceous leaves, in autumn it shifts entirely to a diet of conifer needles. This shift to a single-item diet, accompanied by the increasing use of trees for both roosting and feeding, begins well before the arrival of snow cover and continues throughout winter even in the absence of snow.

**WATER SHREW *(Sorex palustris)***
Found mainly along wooded streams with dense vegetative cover and shelter of rocks, stumps, or logs. Feeds primarily on aquatic invertebrates, but also on small fish, snails, terrestrial invertebrates, and earthworms. Weighs less than half an ounce and may be preyed upon by trout when diving for food.

**SOUTHERN RED-BACKED VOLE *(Clethrionomys gapperi)*** Active day or night, year-round, preferring habitat with abundant stumps, rotting logs, and downed trees. Opportunistic feeders on all plant material, fungi, and arthropods. Remain active in winter under the snow, where their foraging area may exceed their summertime home range.

**DEER MOUSE *(Peromyscus maniculatus)*** Most widespread and morphologically variable mouse in North America. All subspecies have large, black bulging eyes; relatively large, naked ears; and a sharply bicolored tail, dark above and white beneath. A true habitat and feeding generalist; at home in trees as well as on the ground.

**SHORT-TAILED WEASEL (*Mustela erminea*)** Primarily nocturnal, but often seen during the day in winter. An energetic hunter of small mammals, their numbers fluctuate as populations of prey species rise and fall. Family groups are sometimes seen together as females teach young how to hunt.

**RED SQUIRREL (*Tamiasciurus hudsonicus*)** Found in coniferous forests across the continent (occasionally in hardwood forests at the edge of its range in the southern Appalachians). Active during the day, feeding mostly on conifer seeds, but also on insects, birds' eggs, small vertebrates, and mushrooms, some of which are toxic to humans.

**SNOWSHOE HARE (*Lepus americanus*)** Named for its disproportionately large hind feet, enabling efficient travel over deep snow. Moves to and from feeding sites on well-used runways, browsing by night on conifer needles, shrubs, and succulent vegetation. Beds under dense conifers or downed trees during the day. Also attracted to carrion in winter.

**AMERICAN MARTEN (*Martes americana*)** Active day and night; an adept hunter in trees, as well as on the ground. Preys heavily on red-backed voles, but all small mammals, including flying squirrels and snowshoe hares, are potential prey. Will also eat insects, fruits, and seeds in summer.

**NORTH AMERICAN PORCUPINE (*Erethizon dorsatum*)** Feeds on a variety of succulent plants during summer, switching to the inner bark of trees during winter. Favors hemlock in the Northeast, but also feeds on white pine, balsam fir, maple, and beech. Travels through snow with great difficulty, but shows a remarkable tolerance to cold.

**AMERICAN BEAVER (*Castor canadensis*)** A keystone species in northern freshwater environments, affecting local hydrology, nutrient cycling, and plant succession, and creating a mosaic of habitat patches for other animals. Favored foods include the inner bark of willows and aspen.

**CANADA LYNX (Lynx canadensis)**
An animal of deep woods, deep snow, and deep cold. Large, spreading, well-furred paws are reminiscent of the snowshoe hare, upon which the lynx depends heavily. Now extirpated from the Adirondack region and listed as endangered in Vermont and New Hampshire.

**BLACK BEAR (Ursus americanus)**
Found throughout the boreal forest and south along Appalachians. Color variable but in the Northeast mostly black with a brown muzzle. Omnivorous and adaptable; will prey upon newborn mammals and birds, though bulk of diet consists of fruits, nuts, and vegetation. Also raids ant colonies for pupae. Young born in winter den.

**MOOSE (Alces alces)** Widely distributed throughout the boreal forests of North America and Eurasia. Restricted to cool regions due to its large size, bacterial heat production in the rumen, and inability to perspire. Adults may consume more than 40 pounds per day of leaves and aquatic plants in summer, and woody twigs in winter.

**PINE GROSBEAK (*Pinicola enucleator*)** A seed and fruit generalist in conifer and hardwood forests, favoring pine seeds, mountain ash berries, and maple buds. Nests in conifers; male feeds female as part of courtship ritual. Year-round resident in Adirondacks and northern New England, breeding as far north as treeline in Canada. Easy to approach in winter.

**RED-BREASTED NUTHATCH (*Sitta canadensis*)** Year-round resident in northern coniferous forests, preferring mature forests with decaying trees for nest sites. Gleans insects from small branches and outer twigs, but may consume many conifer seeds in winter. Pairs sometimes remain together through winter if sufficient food is available.

**PINE SISKIN (*Carduelis pinus*)** Gregarious and frequently flocking with goldfinches, juncos, and crossbills, especially in fall and winter. Feeds on seeds, buds, floral nectar, and tree sap. Often semi-colonial, nesting within a few feet of each other. Found year-round in the northern forest, but some may migrate as far south as Florida.

**WHITE-WINGED CROSSBILL (Loxia leucoptera)** Bold, white wingbars distinguish this species from the red crossbill. Feeds on conifer seeds by forcing bill between cone scales and prying the scales open while lifting seed out with its tongue. Acts much like a small parrot while feeding, using both bill and feet to move among branch tips.

**GRAY JAY (Perisoreus canadensis)** Highly opportunistic feeder, not shy about taking handouts from hikers or raiding campsites. In addition to its regular diet of insects, fruit, and carrion, will also rob other birds' eggs and prey on nestlings. Remains within its breeding range all winter, but may migrate to lower elevations in fall.

**YELLOW-RUMPED WARBLER (Dendroica coronata)** Mostly migratory, but some overwinter along the north Atlantic coast, where they subsist on the waxy berries of myrtle and bayberry shrubs. A generalist insectivore that explores every dimension of its breeding habitat for food, even skimming swallow-like over water for insects.

### BLACK-THROATED GREEN WARBLER *(Dendroica virens)*
Migrant that winters in the Bahamas, Cuba, Jamaica, and Central America. Gleans insects from leaves, sometimes hovering to pick them off the undersides. Male sings persistently during the breeding season with one of the most recognizable songs in the northern forest—a buzzed *zee-zee-zee-zoo-zee.*

### BLACKPOLL WARBLER *(Dendroica striata)* A common insectivore preferring spruce trees for breeding. Its autumn migration between the northern forest and South America requires a non-stop flight of some 1,800 miles over water, taking an estimated 88 hours. Prior to departure, it doubles its weight with energy reserves.

### BLACKBURNIAN WARBLER *(Dendroica fusca)* The only North American warbler with a fiery orange throat. Difficult to observe during breeding due to its habit of singing, nesting, and foraging in the highest tops of conifers. Reported to join foraging flocks of chickadees, nuthatches, and kinglets after fledging, its begging young following along.

### WHITE-THROATED SPARROW

*(Zonotrichia albicollis)* A familiar songster of the northern forest, sometimes singing through the night. Nests and feeds mostly near the ground in dense vegetation right up to treeline. Primarily a seed eater but feeds its young almost entirely animal matter. Winters mostly in the mid-Atlantic and southern states.

### GOLDEN-CROWNED KINGLET

*(Regulus satrapa)* Only slightly larger than a hummingbird and almost continuously active in spruce-fir forests. Female starts second brood immediately after first young leave the nest. Male feeds the fledglings, the incubating female, and itself. Many overwinter in the northern forest, gleaning insects from tree bark.

### NORTHERN SAW-WHET OWL

*(Aegolius acadicus)* Uncommon year-round resident that mostly inhabits dense, coniferous bottom lands. Smallest owl in eastern United States; named for the resemblance of its monotonous, raspy call to the sound of sharpening a saw. Strictly nocturnal, feeding on small rodents, especially deer mice, and occasional insects.

The high cellulose and lignin content of conifer needles, combined with their high concentration of plant defense compounds, presents some significant digestive challenges to the spruce grouse, but the bird can handle it. To accommodate this seasonal shift in diet, the digestive tract of the grouse undergoes a remarkable adjustment, wherein the size of the bird's crop (food storage pouch), gizzard (a second stomach where food is ground), large intestine, and caecum (a fermentation chamber with high concentrations of bacterial flora) all increase significantly in size. This is accompanied by an important behavioral adaptation, as well—a drive to seek out and ingest grit (sand or gravel) found along roads, stream banks, or uprooted trees, as it apparently improves the grinding of coarse fibrous needles in the gizzard. In autumn, experienced grouse will make deliberate overland excursions of considerable distance to familiar sources of grit, where they may congregate with others for several days before finally dispersing to their wintering territories.

While this unusual diet, with its low digestibility and low protein content, requires considerably greater food intake during the cold season, the spruce grouse is assured a virtually unlimited supply of food throughout winter, expending very little energy to obtain it.

## HEATH BOGS

Here and there, the spruce-fir forests open up into treeless glades—an old beaver meadow, perhaps, where grasses and sedges have colonized the mud flats behind a broken dam, or a bog where heath shrubs and sphagnum moss have woven a dense mat of vegetation over still water. A certain sense of excitement comes with unexpectedly encountering these backwaters of the boreal forest—an excitement spurred by the anticipation of finding a rare orchid or surprising a cow moose and her calf browsing on pond weeds. It's a just anticipation, because these open areas are uncommon habitats, and uncommon habitats often hold rare sights.

The orchid and the moose are not always found in the same place, however, for their natural preferences differ, and there are several important distinctions between the marsh flooded by beaver activity, where we are likely to see the moose, and a heath bog, where we are apt to find the orchid. In fact, in many respects the two habitats are quite opposite. The marsh is richer in nutrients and therefore supports much more productive plant growth, and it often teems with wildlife—mammals, birds, amphibians, and fish. The bog, on the other hand, is nutrient poor and highly acidic, so that only a relatively few plant species live there, and its animal life is mostly transient, finding little reason to take up residence. That both of these wetland types may develop within the same stretch of boreal forest, though, compels us to ask what makes for such differences in physical and biological nature between the two habitats. Why is it that some wet spots become marshes or swamps and others bogs?

The character of a wetland is determined in large part by the amount of groundwater circulating through it. Moving water brings in more nutrients than still water either because it increases the importation of minerals from outside the area or because it increases contact between water and soil particles, aiding in nutrient exchange. Improved nutrient relations generally mean more species, greater productivity (that is, more solar energy captured by plants), and more energy moving through the food web. The most fundamental difference between a marsh and a bog, then, has to do with groundwater movement. Bogs develop where groundwater circulation is blocked, where flow-through is negligible, and where nutrients come primarily—sometimes entirely—from rainwater. Marshes, on the other hand, always have some water circulation, however imperceptible it may be. Even if water has been impounded by beavers, flow-through is sufficient to maintain a higher nutrient status than in a bog.

These conditions translate into distinct differences between the two wetlands in soil type and plant cover. The soils of bogs consist entirely of undecomposed organic matter, reflecting a general lack of microbial activity, and it is often possible to identify plant remains several hundred years old. In contrast, the rate of decomposition in marshes is more rapid and, although marsh soil is richly organic, it contains little of recognizable plant remains. The vegetation supported by these two wetland types is strikingly different too, and one can tell at a glance what is going on beneath the surface just by the presence or absence of a few key species. Cattails in standing water always indicate nutrient enrichment, whereas a preponderance of evergreen shrubs and sphagnum moss around the water's edge indicates a low-nutrient environment (see Figures 9 and 10b).

Many of the bogs we encounter in the northern Appalachians have floating mats of vegetation. Called "quaking" bogs, these formed in water-filled kettle holes left by the disappearance of glacial ice buried within deep gravel deposits. The development of a quaking bog over open water in these kettles does not depend on sedimentation and basin filling, as is often the case with a marsh, but rather involves the progressive development over a period of centuries of vegetation that floats over the water, accumulates organic matter, and builds in thickness downward from the water's surface. The primary mat-forming species in our area is leatherleaf, a woody shrub that commonly invades still water and pond shores (see Figure 10a). As this plant branches out over the open water, the increasing weight of foliage depresses the older branches below the water's surface, stimulating new shoot growth and forming a dense tangle of branches. In a similar fashion, sweet gale and buckbean may also weave a mat over the water. The accumulation of litter on this framework of branches eventually creates a floating substrate (underlying layer) suitable for colonization

**FIGURE 9** Differences in vegetative character between bogs and marshes are determined largely by nutrient availability, which in turn is affected by groundwater circulation. Both the open-water channel in this marsh and the alders and grasses lining the channel tell of improved nutrient relations.

by other plants. This often begins with sphagnum moss and a few species of aquatic sedges that are tolerant of acidic conditions. Pitcher plants and sundew may then follow, and as consolidation of the mat progresses with the accumulation of sphagnum peat, other heath shrubs become established (see Figure 10b). By this time in the bog's succession, the mat will usually hold the weight of an adult person, but it will quiver as you walk across it, like a giant waterbed, and will remain a "quaking" bog until it finally fills to the bottom with organic matter and becomes solid.

The invasion of a wet site by leatherleaf does not, by itself, set the direction of succession. If physical influences like fluctuating water levels or a change in nutrient status favors the growth of floating pond weeds or emergent aquatic vegetation, the site might still develop into a marsh. However, once sphagnum mosses become established, the direction of succession becomes irrevocably set, provided that no significant outside influences intervene. This is because sphagnum moss (see Figure 11a), more than any other species, reinforces all those conditions that make a bog what it is. For one thing, sphagnum has an extraordinary capacity to retain water. It is so absorbent that it has long been used by indigenous people in the North as a natural diaper material. In addition, sphagnum moss has a rapid growth rate and accumulates very quickly in the bog because it decomposes so slowly. This combination of rapid accumulation and high absorptive capacity means that sphagnum helps retain water and greatly reduces its movement through the bog.

But perhaps the most important influence of sphagnum moss in directing succession lies in its ability to acidify the environment in which it grows. Sphagnum has an extraordinary capacity to exchange positively charged atoms in the bog water, absorbing nutrients like calcium and replacing them with hydrogen ions, leaving the water acidified in the process. (Acidity, remember, is a measure of hydrogen ion concentration.) The resulting acidity inhibits microbial activity and reduces nutrient availability, leaving some plants to supplement nutrients by capturing insects (see Figure 11b). I have seen situations where the open water at the center of a bog was actually alkaline, with a pH of 8.0, while less than 30 feet away, where sphagnum was invading the floating mat, the pH was down to 3.8—acidic enough to preserve anything that might fall into it! Thus sphagnum, in effect, inhibits its own decomposition.

**FIGURE 10** Leatherleaf growing in open water (a) creates a dense tangle of branches that traps litter, eventually forming a floating mat upon which other plants become rooted. Behind the leading edge of leatherleaf, sphagnum moss and sedges take hold to give the bog its unique character (b).

**FIGURE 11** Sphagnum moss (a) is of overriding influence in the development of a bog, largely through its role in acidifying the soil and rendering many nutrients insoluble. Round-leaved sundew (b) deals with nutrient impoverishment by capturing insects to supplement its nutrient intake.

## Double-Dealing Plants

NO OTHER PLANT that I can think of epitomizes adaptation in the natural world quite like the pitcher plant. Within the vat of its highly evolved leaves, this plant harbors its own living microcosm, a miniature ecosystem, superimposed on the stingy substrate of the sphagnum bog.

The pitcher plant obtains its energy through photosynthesis, but like all green plants, it must extract nutrients from the soil or rainwater to build protein and other essential plant compounds. The bog, we know, is not very generous in this regard, but the pitcher plant has found two ways to overcome the problem of nutrient shortage.

The adaptation that we are most familiar with is its insectivorous habit. Beneath its liver-colored flowers (said to attract carrion-feeding insects) the plant lays an eloquent trap. In the course of evolution its leaves have curled and fused to form a receptacle that arches gracefully upward to catch rainwater; but it is not water alone that the plant consumes. These unique leaves are equipped with their own nectaries to attract insects and with other devices to ensure that once attracted, the visitors will not leave again. Hundreds of downward-pointing hairs around the lip of the leaf make it easy for an insect to descend into the pitcher but nearly impossible for it to crawl back out against the grain. Below the throat of the pitcher, epidermal cells exude a sticky substance and slough off easily, attaching to the insect's feet and further inhibiting its escape. The struggling insect slips into the water at the bottom of the

pitcher and soon drowns, to be digested through the actions of enzymes the plant secretes into the water.

The insectivorous habit of this and other plants of similar environments, including sundew, provides an important supplement to the scant supply of nitrogen in a bog. But the pitcher plant does not leave nutrient procurement only to the chance capture of insects. Within the body of water held in the leaf, thriving populations of bacteria grow, their entire world contained in that little vat of enriched rainwater. Recent studies have shown that nitrogen-fixing bacteria, those with the special ability to convert atmospheric nitrogen to a form suitable for plant uptake, are regular constituents of the pitcher's aquatic community, and that the levels of nitrogen found in leaf tissues of the pitcher plant could be accounted for by bacterial activity alone.

Thus the pitcher's little world is a much more complicated system than meets the eye. Close observation reveals still more going on within this microcosm, where many other organisms take advantage of the pitcher plant's unique adaptations. It has been found, for example, that one species of mosquito actually breeds in the water within the leaf, its larvae maturing there before taking flight as winged adults; that a small moth also lays its eggs exclusively on the pitcher plant so that its larvae can mature within the protection of the newly developing leaf cavities while actually feeding on the interior epidermal cells; and that some species of spiders spin webs across the opening of the pitcher to intercept insects destined to nourish one or the other, plant or spider. So should you encounter a pitcher plant, take a few minutes to examine a leaf closely, without disturbing it. You may witness a lot of drama within this miniature ecosystem.

---

Eventually, scattered individuals of black spruce and tamarack may become established on the mature bog mat (see Figure 12), but the question is still open as to whether or not succession will proceed in the end to a spruce-fir forest community. The number of plants that can tolerate the conditions of the bog habitat is so limited that species replacement, as we have described in floristic relay succession, does not occur on the mat. And recently, it has been discovered that one of the common bog shrubs, sheep laurel, releases a chemical that specifically inhibits root development in black spruce. It seems that this one plant, and perhaps others yet to be discovered, protects its own interests and contributes further to the bog's longevity.

Not all bogs originate in kettle holes. Some may form in shallow bedrock depressions at high elevations where rainfall provides adequate moisture to

**FIGURE 12** Bog succession follows its own set of rules. This small tamarack is ahead of its time, as the successful invasion of trees must await basin filling and solidification of the organic substrate beneath the floating mat.

support bog vegetation. Perhaps the most numerous and extensive of these are found along the ridge tops of the Mahoosuc Range, on the Maine–New Hampshire border (see Figure 13a), where they are couched among drier heath balds. (The origin of the latter, which are plant communities dominated by sheep laurel and other heath shrubs, is not completely understood.) These ridge-top bogs are often colonized first by a moss called *Drepanocladus fluitans* (it has no common name) and by a tussock-forming alpine plant called deer's hair sedge, which seems to prefer wet or disturbed soils (see Figure 13b). This early successional stage may bear little resemblance to the pioneering plant community of low-elevation bogs, but these two species pave the way for others like the round-leaved sundew and the small bog cranberry. Eventually sphagnum moss invades and the bog begins to take on a familiar look. Once sphagnum has become established, the direction of succession is similar to that at low elevations, except for the addition of a few new species like alpine bilberry, black crowberry, and a dwarf raspberry called cloudberry.

**FIGURE 13** Ridge-top bogs (a) in the Mahoosuc Range in Maine develop in shallow bedrock depressions. Colonization by the moss *Drepanocladus fluitans* and the tussock-forming deer's hair sedge (b) paves the way for sphagnum, which then sets the direction of succession.

## The Woolly Leaf Paradox

THAT MANY NORTHERN bog plants should share so much in common with arid land plants seems a striking contradiction, yet the thick waxy leaves of leatherleaf and sheep laurel, the narrow rolled-under leaves of bog rosemary and bog laurel, and the dense woolly underside of Labrador tea all represent classic water-conserving adaptations. Each of these features is designed to increase the resistance of the leaf to the outward diffusion of water vapor, thereby reducing water loss when the supply

Labrador tea

is limited. The obvious question, then, is why, when they are growing with their roots in water, do these plants display such adaptations?

For many decades this question led ecologists to hypothesize a condition of physiological drought in bogs, suggesting that even though water appears plentiful, it is not available to the plants. The reason, they speculated, is somehow related to the high acidity and low oxygen content of the bog water, which perhaps inhibits root uptake. However, studies made possible by more recent technological advances have disproved most of these hypotheses, and it now appears that water conservation may be important to these plants only secondarily.

The one other characteristic that these bog plants share is that they are evergreen, and evergreen leaves, as described in "The Evergreen Advantage" on page 42, are adaptive in nutrient-deficient environments where their longevity results in a greater yield of photosynthate per unit of nutrient invested in their construction. Few environments are as nutrient deficient as bogs, for input is limited almost entirely to rainwater—not a particularly rich source—and the high acidity of the bog further reduces the availability of some elements. But life is full of trade-offs, and the big risk that the evergreen plant faces is excessive water loss from sun-exposed foliage during winter, when the supply of water from cold or frozen soils is limited. This is where the water-conserving adaptations play a role. In bog plants, then, the evergreen habit is apparently the primary adaptation—a nutrient-conservation strategy—and water-conserving adaptations are a secondary means of getting the evergreen leaf safely through the winter.

The principal sphagnum species in these subalpine bogs is *Sphagnum fuscum* (no common name), which is leather-brown in color and has very small, tightly clustered leaves that give it a manicured and cushiony appearance. This species, too, has a very rapid growth rate, considering the environment it lives in, and nearly engulfs the other plants that grow in the bog with it. In fact, where the bog is dominated by *Sphagnum fuscum*, the heath shrubs appear much smaller than usual and provide only sparse ground cover; poking beneath the surface, though, reveals that these are not dwarfed shrubs at all, but rather only the very tips of branches reaching for daylight. Whole plants, buried by the sphagnum, are just managing to keep a few leaves above the surface. The moss layer rises almost one-half inch each year, and the growth rate of the other plants barely matches that!

In the subalpine bogs of the higher ridge tops, *Sphagnum fuscum* is responsible for yet another interesting feature—the preservation of frozen lenses of peat beneath the surface. These windswept ridges are blown clear of snow throughout much of the winter, and without that protective cover, soils freeze right to bedrock. When the thick sphagnum cushion dries at the surface during the following summer, it becomes a very good insulator and keeps the peat beneath from thawing completely. The frozen lenses may persist throughout the summer and into the fall, perhaps lasting year-round in some cases, and no doubt have a very important influence on succession in these bogs. Apart from inhibiting nutrient-cycling processes, such cold soils would surely impair root development for any invading conifer seedlings. So again we find that these bog habitats are very stable, largely through the self-perpetuating role of sphagnum.

While I suggested earlier that in bogs, birds and mammals are mostly transients, there are two interesting exceptions in the northern forest. The first, the northern bog lemming, is a small vole-like mammal (quite similar in appearance to our common red-backed vole, but with a blunt nose and grayer coat) most often associated with deep, moist sphagnum moss where it constructs nests of dry leaves and occasionally fur, sometimes several inches below the surface. It makes frequent use of runways in the dense litter layer and feeds on the leafy sedges, grasses, seeds, and some fungi. This is yet another species that is widespread in Canada and Alaska, but reaches its southern range limit in northern New England. Even though it is a social animal, highly interactive with other members of its species, the northern bog lemming is not found in large numbers anywhere within its range. In the northeastern United States it is rare and local, not unlike its specialized habitat, and is restricted to a few locations in northernmost Maine and New Hampshire.

Another bog "specialist" is the palm warbler (named for its close association with palm trees in its Florida and Caribbean wintering grounds). While several birds of our spruce-fir woodlands may nest in close proximity to bogs, especially those like the Cape May warbler that prefer more open settings or conifer forest edges, the palm warbler actually prefers to be in the bog. Its cup-shaped nest is constructed of a variety of materials—plant stalks, rootlets, bark shreds, sedges, and ferns—and is often situated right in the sphagnum moss at the base of a small conifer, or on a dry hummock where it is concealed by sedges and heath shrubs. The palm warbler forages mostly on the ground, its diet comprised almost exclusively of insects. Like the northern bog lemming, this warbler breeds mostly to the north in Canada, and its distribution in New England is limited to the heath bogs of northern Maine and New Hampshire.

## NORTHERN HARDWOOD FORESTS

How much poorer would we be without deciduous broadleaf forests; without their spring show of ephemeral wildflowers and their cool green summer shade; without the exuberance of their fall colors, the smell of dried leaves, and that sense of season that keeps us in touch with the rhythms of the natural world? And when the leaves are down and the skies gray with the first snows of November, these same hardwoods—the sugar maple, beech, and yellow birch—keep us warm around the woodstove, for no conifer gives back as much heat in winter.

The deciduous forests add much to the diversity of our landscape. These are the forests of deeper, better-drained soils; forests of the middle ground between the extremes of the cold, wet bottom lands and the rocky, wind-swept subalpine slopes; forests that harbor a wealth of plant and animal species that find the coniferous woods lacking for one reason or another.

The sugar maple and beech that dominate these woodlands are not unique to the Northeast; their ranges actually go far south, extending all the way down the Appalachians and the Mississippi Valley into Georgia and Arkansas. But in the northern Appalachians these two species, together with yellow birch, form a distinctive community that we call the "northern hardwood association." Of course these species are not alone in this community. Other maples—striped or goosefoot, mountain, and red—along with black and pin cherry, white ash, and paper birch are also common in the mature northern hardwood forest. And it is not a community of hardwoods only, as the name suggests. White pine is scattered widely about, a persistent remnant of earlier successional stages, often seen silhouetted against the skyline as on many lower ridge tops in the Adirondacks. Hemlock and red spruce are important constituents of these woods too, perhaps even more so in earlier days than in our present second- or third-growth forests; and in many places today balsam fir can be seen establishing itself in the understory. By and large, though, sugar maple, beech, and yellow birch dominate the northern hardwood forests and give them that special character for which much of the Adirondack and northern New England region is so well known.

It is to a large extent the seasonality of these three deciduous trees that sets the tempo of life in the northern hardwood forests. For many of the small perennials of the forest floor, the growing season is compressed between the time when snow cover disappears and the days when the hardwood canopy closes over with new summer leaves. The forest canopy acts as a filter affecting not just the quantity of light reaching the forest floor, but also its quality, its suitability for photosynthesis. For many of the ephemeral herbs, springtime is a race to complete their life cycle before light becomes too limited. Some species even begin their growth under the snowpack, channeling last year's starch reserves into new tissue and manufacturing chlorophyll under the weak blue light that filters down through the snow. The familiar trout lily and spring beauty are among the first of the ephemeral herbs to appear, sometimes flowering within a couple of days after being released from the snowpack. But barely six weeks later the plants can scarcely be found, for they have done what they were programmed to do and have put away sufficient carbohydrate in their underground corms to carry them through to another spring.

The hardwood trees themselves are geared for maximum energy conversion during a relatively short growing season. If the evergreen conifer is likened to a long-term enterprise, using resources conservatively for a return over a longer period, then the deciduous broadleaf tree is the opportunist looking for a quick return on its investment. The deciduous hardwood must produce its entire photosynthetic machinery anew each year and must get sufficient return from it not only to pay back the energy costs of construction and maintenance but also to support new growth of the tree. And because the hardwood tree sheds its leaves each fall, it has to store enough carbohydrates during the summer to support the flush of new leaves the following year. Unlike the conifer, the hardwood has no older foliage from which it can borrow photosynthetic reserves to fuel the spring start-up. The tree is equal to its task, however. Compared to the evergreen leaf, the hardwood leaf generally has a thinner wax coating (a benefit of not having to protect itself all winter) and many more stomates, the tiny pores through which carbon dioxide and water vapor pass. It is therefore nearly ten times more efficient than the conifer needle in obtaining atmospheric carbon dioxide for photosynthesis. What the hardwood leaf lacks in longevity, it seems to make up for in increased photosynthetic efficiency. Its ability to produce surplus energy reserves is evidenced by the presence of large stores of sugars that are mobilized and translocated to budding shoots as the days of spring warm above freezing. Stores can be tapped for syrup production with little effect on the tree. It is noteworthy that the healthy hardwood tree generally produces enough of a surplus to withstand one or two complete defoliations from insect infestation before it runs out of reserves. And all of this reserve energy is accumulated during a growing season of at best three months.

I noted in the opening chapter that the present expansiveness of northern hardwood forests in upstate New York and northern New England is due in large part to logging activity in this region. Although something of an artifact in many locations, these forests nonetheless are very stable communities on the better-drained sites throughout the northern Appalachians. Many opportunistic species in this community quickly fill and stabilize small openings in the forest, and because the community dominants are shade tolerant they are able to maintain themselves for a long time. The notion of stability, though, should not conjure up images of static forests, never changing in composition under the closed canopy. The three forest dominants (beech, yellow birch, and sugar maple) themselves differ markedly in their reproductive strategies, so that over time their position relative to each other changes. Yellow birch is the most mobile of the group (as is paper birch at the higher elevations), producing large quantities of very light seeds that get around the forest quite well. And when the opportunity arises—when an old giant of a sugar maple finally crashes to the ground—the yellow birch seed is there and germinates quickly in the new opening. Skid roads from logging operations often provide an ideal seed bed for birch, and on the distant hillsides one can often see thin lines of a different green extending into the spruce woods as yellow birch and paper birch record the history of logging activity for the discerning eye to recognize. Within the hardwood forests, then, the distribution of yellow birch is often patchy and the patches shift about over time because yellow birch does not reproduce as well in its own shade as do the other dominants.

Beech is much less opportunistic than yellow birch in its reproductive strategy. Instead of releasing large quantities of mobile seeds, it produces far fewer and much bigger seeds, commonly called "beech nuts." They don't get around very well, but these seeds store large energy reserves that improve their chances of success where they do germinate, often in the shade of the parent tree. With all their stored food, beech nuts are attractive to many foraging animals—squirrels, wild turkeys, bears—which of course offsets some of their other advantages. However, as if to add a little insurance, the beech has a habit of cloning—producing sprouts from roots—which is an ideal way of holding on to a favorable site. So between their heavy seeds and occasional root sprouting, beech trees, once established, tend to be stable over time in terms of spatial distribution.

This is not to suggest that beech will occupy a given site forever, though. Like all trees, beech may succumb to any number of problems with aging, (see "Beech Bark Disease" on page 73) and other species—the shade-tolerant hemlock and red spruce, for example—marking time nearby, may be ready to grow into a new opening. And invisible but omnipresent seeds of pioneer species often lie buried yet viable until some disturbance like a fire or logging activity removes the organic litter and triggers their germination. Pin cherry, an early colonizer that lives only about 30 years, may produce 5 million seeds per acre from a dense stand, which are then distributed widely by foraging birds. These seeds remain viable in the soil for more than fifteen years and germinate quickly with disturbance, springing up as if through spontaneous generation when no other pin cherries are around. In hardwood stands over 100 years old, where pin cherry has long since disappeared, as many as 40,000 seeds of this species per acre may lie buried in the soil. Red maple, paper birch, and yellow birch, each with seed longevity of up to fifteen years, are also well represented in the buried seed pool of the forest floor, and crop up very quickly after a disturbance. Paper birch, in particular, appears to proliferate after fire, especially at upper elevations, and occasionally a person will come across large and nearly pure stands of this species whose origin was associated with a burn. A look around in the litter layer of these stands will often reveal old fire-scarred stumps or charcoal in the soil.

When we talk about stability in a climax northern hardwood forest we don't mean to imply a static condition. To be sure, the dominant sugar maple, beech, and yellow birch are long-lived and could potentially occupy a site for centuries. But if we could observe a landscape long enough, we would see a slowly continuing internal reorganization, with beech growing up under sugar maple, sugar maple seeding in under yellow birch, and yellow birch reestablishing itself in new openings. The conifers, too—particularly white pine, hemlock, and red spruce—maintain a presence in these forests as local conditions favor their establishment in the understory. The climax northern hardwood forest, then, exists in a sort of fluid equilibrium, always changing, but viewed on a larger scale, always the same.

This dynamic nature of our hardwood forest—its shifting age structure and understory composition over time—has implications for mammal and bird species as well. The relatively high diversity of plant species in our northern hardwood forests, especially in transitional areas where there is some intermingling of boreal elements, coupled with its multistoried structure, translates into more ecological niches for animals to fill. Consequently, mammal diversity tends to be higher in our northern hardwood forests than in the spruce-fir woodlands, particularly since many mammals associated with conifer forests will exploit (or at least pass through) nearby hardwood cover as well. The southern red-backed vole, red fox, northern flying squirrel, porcupine, and white-tailed deer appear equally at home in hardwood and conifer forests. The common denominator for each of these, however, seems to be forest age. With the exception of the porcupine, all tend to prefer

# Beech Bark Disease

MANY OLDER STANDS of beech in the Northeast have suffered serious dieback in recent years, the result of a wave of disease that moved through the area in the 1950s and '60s. Beech bark disease is a pathological condition actually involving two different attack organisms, neither of which by itself would likely cause the death of a tree. The disease starts when tiny, wingless insects collectively called "woolly beech scale" invade a tree, quite often an aging or injured tree, and begin feeding on the bark. These insects resemble aphids in their manner of feeding, inserting a sucking stylet into living bark tissues, and like the aphid, produce a woolly white wax covering that is usually the first visible evidence of their presence. In large numbers, these insects bring about the death of bark tissues as they tap the living cells for metabolites. This condition causes the bark to crack and creates an opportunity for invasion by another organism known as the "canker fungus." This fungus parasitizes the bark tissue too, and may eventually girdle the tree. The conspicuous pink coloring of the bark by numerous tiny red fruiting bodies of the canker fungus is sure evidence that the bark of the tree has been killed. By this point decay fungi may have already entered the wood, perhaps with secondary wood-boring insects, and the weakened bole is susceptible to breakage in the wind, a phenomenon known as beech snap.

Beech scale was accidentally introduced into Nova Scotia on nursery stock from Europe in the late 1800s and has slowly pushed its way south and west. The first wave of beech bark disease had progressed through northern New England and into the Adirondacks by 1960, eventually reaching southern Pennsylvania and western New York State. In the aftermath of the resulting dieback, the abundance of beech in many places has actually increased with saplings that sprouted from the roots of affected trees. Young trees are usually more resistant than older ones, but many of these second-generation thickets, the vegetative progeny of diseased trees, have already become infested with another scale insect, *Xylococculus betulae*, that creates wounds on which the woolly beech scale (now a permanent resident in the Northeast), and later the canker fungus, can get established. Because the woolly beech scale is present throughout the Northeast now and is dispersed primarily by the wind, new local outbreaks of beech bark disease can erupt almost anywhere in the area. Here and there, however, apparently resistant trees have survived the initial wave, which along with the persistent root sprouting of diseased trees, gives hope that the beech will not go the way of the disease-ravaged American chestnut and American elm.

**AMERICAN BEECH**
*(Fagus grandifolia)* Bark hard, relatively smooth and non-flaking, with numerous raised "freckles." Trunk and branches a cool, light gray. Leaves have coarse, saw-tooth margins with parallel veins ending at the tip of each tooth. Large seeds (beech nuts) are consumed by many species of wildlife.

**WHITE ASH** *(Fraxinus americana)* Bark soft, non-scaly, and finely fissured in a diamond-like pattern. Leaves compound, composed of five to nine paired leaflets with one leaflet at the end. Leaf margins smooth or very finely toothed. Wood is strong and straight-grained, traditionally used for making baseball bats, hockey sticks, oars, and shovel handles.

**AMERICAN MOUNTAIN ASH** *(Sorbus americana)*
A small tree in the rose family with compound leaves and large clusters of white flowers. Bright red berries mature in autumn and persist into winter. Bark thin and smooth with prominent lenticels sometimes coalescing into horizontal bands. An important source of fruit for birds, found mostly at higher elevations.

**RED MAPLE** *(Acer rubrum)* Younger trees with smooth, gray bark, becoming rough, irregularly fissured, and flaking with age. Leaves opposite each other on twigs, leaf interlobes V-shaped, and margins sharply toothed. Buds are rounded and clustered at twig ends. Often growing in wet soils, earning the name "swamp maple."

**SUGAR MAPLE (*Acer saccharum)* Bark of young and mature trees similar to red maple. Leaves are opposite each other as with all maples. Interlobes U-shaped, and leaf margins not saw-toothed. Buds small, narrow, and pointed. An important furniture wood and the commercial source of maple syrup and sugar.

**STRIPED MAPLE** *(Acer pensylvanicum)* A small tree, rarely more than 7 inches in diameter. Bark bright green with white stripes when young, turning reddish-brown with paler vertical lines as it ages. Leaves have three broad, sharply pointed lobes suggesting the tree's other name, "goosefoot maple."

**PIN CHERRY (*Prunus pensylvanica*)** Bark lustrous, reddish-brown, tending toward charcoal gray with age. Prominent horizontal lenticels. Leaf margins with tiny teeth curving inward. Pungent odor of crushed leaves and bark confirms identity as a cherry. Also known as "fire cherry" for its vigorous regeneration after a burn.

**BLACK CHERRY** *(Prunus serotina)* Bark reddish-brown to black, scaling and curling outward. Peeling off a curl reveals the pungent odor characteristic of cherry. Leaves also pungent when crushed. Wood reddish-brown, satiny, valued especially for furniture. Wild cherry syrup for cough medicine is extracted from the bark.

**QUAKING ASPEN**
*(Populus tremuloides)*
Bark smooth, light gray-green, becoming dark and deeply furrowed on the lower trunks of old trees. Leaf stems flattened in plane perpendicular to leaf blade causing leaf to flutter in slightest breeze. Most widely distributed tree in North America and an important pioneer species.

**GRAY BIRCH** *(Betula populifolia)* Bark tight and unpeeling; grayish-white, with numerous black lenticels. Leaves triangular, tapering to a long, pointed tip. A somewhat scraggly pioneer species on poor soils and abandoned farmland.

**PAPER BIRCH *(Betula papyrifera)*** Bark of mature trees white to tawny and peels in wide, papery strips. Young trees, particularly at high elevation, may have dark reddish, non-peeling bark with prominent white lenticels. Leaf margins double-toothed (small teeth superimposed on a pattern of larger teeth). Twigs lack wintergreen fragrance of yellow birch.

**YELLOW BIRCH (*Betula alleghaniensis*)** Bark golden or silvery and peels in thin, narrow curls; a good tinder even when wet. Old trees develop rough, scaly bark, but branches and roots still show smooth, gold color. Leaves double-toothed. Freshly broken twigs have a wintergreen fragrance.

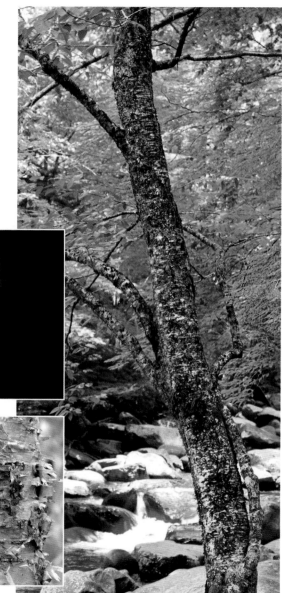

**BLOODROOT** *(Sanguinaria canadensis)*
Named for its orange-red sap. Grows from a rhizome, with leaf and flower each on a separate stem. Sap from rhizome used by American Indians as a dye for baskets, clothing, and face paint, and as a mosquito repellent. Sap extremely toxic; possibly fatal if ingested in large dose.

**DUTCHMAN'S BREECHES** *(Dicentra cuculllaria)* Waxy, pantaloon-shaped flowers rise above deeply cut, fern-like leaves. May cause mild and temporary skin irritation when touched. All parts are toxic when ingested in large quantities; contains an alkaloid that depresses the central nervous system.

**FOAMFLOWER** *(Tiarella cordifolia)*
Small, delicate flowers with long, slender stamens impart an airy, foam-like appearance. Genus name is derived from Greek "tiara," meaning turban, referring to shape of the pistil. "Cordifolia" implies heart-shaped foliage, though leaves are more reminiscent of maple.

**JACK-IN-THE-PULPIT (*Arisaema triphyllum*)** Flowers minute and contained within the hooded sheath, or spathe. Mature fruits tightly clustered and bright red and are revealed when the spathe falls away. All parts contain calcium oxalate crystals, producing a strong burning sensation if tasted raw. Tuber edible if dried thoroughly and cooked.

**RED TRILLIUM (*Trillium erectum*)** The crimson red flower standing above a single whorl of diamond-shaped leaves is distinctive. Flower is foul-smelling and attracts carrion flies as pollinators, giving the plant its other name, "stinking Benjamin." Young, unfolding leaves edible raw or cooked.

**ROUND-LOBED HEPATICA (*Hepatica nobilis*)** Blooms early spring on 4- to 6-inch leafless stalks. Leaves arise from ground on separate stems after flowers have opened. Botanical name derived from Greek *hepar,* meaning liver, for resemblance of basal leaves to shape of the human liver.

**HOBBLEBUSH** *(Viburnam lantanoides)*
Shrub up to several feet in height. Long, horizontal branches often intertwine with those of neighboring plants; also take root when in contact with ground, making it difficult to bushwack through, hence the name "hobblebush." Flowers produce bright red berries in fall.

**TROUT LILY** *(Erythronium americanum)*
An early spring ephemeral, often starting its growth beneath the snowpack. Mottled leaves suggest the coloration of brown or brook trout. Roots, leaves, and flowers are considered edible, but are also said to cause vomiting.

**PINK LADY'S SLIPPER** *(Cypripedium acaule)* Large orchid found in a variety of woodland habitats, sometimes in surprising abundance. Latin name translates as Venus's sandal or slipper. Hairs on leaf can cause an allergic reaction similar to poison ivy in some people. The root has antispasmodic and sedative properties.

**RUFFED GROUSE (*Bonasa umbelluss*)** Strongly dependent upon aspen in mixed forests. Diet mostly of buds, leaves, flowers, fruits, and seeds, with some insects. Male heard in early spring "drumming", to attract a mate by flapping its cupped wings forcefully, creating a deep, thumping sound that rapidly accelerates in speed.

**AMERICAN REDSTART (*Setophaga ruticilla*)** Migrant from West Indies and South America, found mostly in second-growth hardwood forests with abundant shrub cover. Flashes bright wing and tail patches to startle insects. Catches insects in midair (its closest competitor may be the least flycatcher) or gleans insects from foliage.

**HERMIT THRUSH (*Catharsus guttatus*)** Secretive bird of mid-elevation coniferous or mixed forests. Nests and feeds on the ground in relatively moist locations, scratching in the litter layer for insects. Repeatedly lifts tail quickly and lowers it slowly. Song is melodic and flute-like.

**WOOD THRUSH *(Hylochichla mustelina)*** A bird of deep woods, with habits similar to hermit thrush. Nests on low branch of tree or shrub, rather than ground. Song described as flute-like and liquid, with each phrase ending in a trill. Has been experiencing steady, long-term declines in number throughout its range.

**EASTERN WOOD PEWEE *(Contopus virens)*** Common but indistinct bird of deciduous forests. Identified by its repeated, slow, plaintive *pee-ah-wee* song. Exploits the middle understory, where it flits out from a perch to catch flying insects and returns to the same perch. Winters in South America.

**WHITE-BREASTED NUTHATCH *(Sitta carolinensis)*** Hardwood forest counterpart of the red-breasted nuthatch. Gleans bark for insects, frequently descending branches and tree trunks upside down. Occasionally searches the ground for insects or seeds. Caches seeds in bark crevices for winter, often covering food with lichens, moss, or snow.

younger forest stands with numerous seedlings and saplings in the understory. A number of other mammals, however, show distinct affinities for the hardwood forest, some shunning the conifer forests altogether. The southern flying squirrel (whose high numbers in our hardwood forests are often surprising) might be the best example of the latter. However, the white-footed mouse, woodland jumping mouse, eastern chipmunk, eastern cottontail, and gray fox are also strongly tied to our northern hardwood forests.

A considerable number of songbirds show strong fidelity to northern hardwood forests, as well. The majority of breeding birds during summer—90 percent or more—are migrants, representing some 30 different species that travel northward from the New World tropics. The species list for any particular location, however, will again depend in part on the successional stage of the forest. We have already seen the importance of this to year-round residents like the wild turkey and ruffed grouse (page 33), the former a bird of mature hardwood forests and the latter a bird of early successional aspen stands. Thus it would not be surprising to learn that migratory birds may be similarly affected by forest condition. Populations of the American redstart, for example, have been shown to be highly correlated with young forest stands, and occur less commonly as forest stands mature. Likewise, the veery is more common in earlier successional (and wetter) sites than its close relative the wood thrush, which shows a preference for interior, mid-successional hardwood forests with substantial undergrowth. Least flycatchers become less abundant as the forest canopy closes in; the ground-foraging ovenbird prefers mature hardwood forests with sparse undergrowth; the hermit thrush prefers a greater mix of conifers than the others; and so on. Habitat selection such as this may be driven in part by competition for space, or by the different feeding habits of birds. Habitat preferences may also change with local circumstances, as close competitors come into or drop out of the picture. For example, habitat preferences among the three thrushes above are similar enough that each is likely to expand its territory in the absence of the other nearby.

Where birds of a given habitat also share dietary preferences, direct competition may be avoided through spatial separation in their feeding or through different feeding behaviors, sometimes aimed at different insect groups. The least flycatcher flits out from a perch to catch flying insects, while the eastern wood pewee, also a flycatcher, feeds by hovering and picking insects off plants above the ground. This is not to suggest that competition is avoided altogether. The white-breasted nuthatch, a year-round resident, gleans insects from the bark of trees, but so does the migratory black-and-white warbler. The latter, however, also picks insects off leaves or intercepts them in air, which nuthatches rarely do. Nuthatches, on the other hand, unlike warblers, will also eat seeds and large nuts that they jam into a bark crevice and hammer open with their bills.

Thus, in many ways the breeding birds of our northern forest find ways to minimize competition and to coexist during the brief but intensive summer season. In so doing, these birds glean myriad insects from the forest, many of which can and do become major defoliators when left unchecked. The departure of these migrants in late summer and fall can also have implications for the future of our forests. In preparation for migration, many of these insectivores turn to seeds and berries, carbohydrate-rich sources of energy to fuel their long flights south, and in so doing disperse some fraction of the seeds to locations where they might one day find conditions suitable for their establishment. The migrants are not without help in this regard, however, for many winter residents are seed eaters as well. In years when birch, beech, and pin cherry produce bumper crops, even birds normally associated with the spruce-fir woodlands—pine siskins, redpolls, and evening grosbeaks—will be drawn into the northern hardwoods, further spreading the seeds of tomorrow's forest. Just as plants affect the distribution of birds, birds affect the distribution of plants.

When you walk through the northern hardwoods now, take note of what is going on in the understory. Is the forest multistoried, consisting of trees of all sizes, as if undisturbed for a long period of time? Are there any remnants of pioneering species still around, for example, old aspen trees? (You will have to look closely because the familiar silver-green bark of the young aspen becomes dark and deeply furrowed in old age.) Are the saplings in the understory of the same species as the overstory trees, or are they different species, perhaps even conifers?

If the forest is not multistoried, are the trees all approximately the same size, suggesting an even-aged stand that might have started with widespread disturbance? Are there any old stumps that suggest a clear-cutting operation, or old blowdowns to suggest wind damage? Is there any evidence of fire, such as bits of charcoal lying on top of the mineral soil or charred stumps and logs? Do the overstory species themselves suggest the nature of the disturbance? Extensive stands of paper birch sometimes follow a burn. Yellow birch and pin cherry often crop up in lines where the mineral soil has been exposed by old logging trails. And while you are hiking in these forests, look for "bear trees." Black bears are crazy about beech nuts, and when they climb beech trees to forage they leave claw marks on the smooth gray bark that callous over and remain visible for years.

## SUBALPINE FORESTS

At elevations above 2,500 feet, the hardwood forest undergoes a rapid transition and climbing farther is like a fast trip north. The changes seen over the next 1,000 vertical feet mimic those that would be seen by driving several hundred miles farther north. Already the red maple, black cherry, white ash, and hemlock of the lower hardwood association have disappeared, and the beech is dropping out quickly. Sugar maple is becoming less common too, and yellow birch is beginning to give way to increasing numbers of paper birch. The red spruce that comprised a minor part of the lower hardwood forests is beginning to grow more thickly now, and mountain ash, a faithful indicator of the changes to come at still higher elevations, has already made its appearance here and there. The forest is starting to take on a more northern or boreal character.

These changes are not a response to increasing elevation *per se*—that is, trees do not respond directly to a reduction in atmospheric pressure. Rather, the changes are a response to the decrease in temperature, with its myriad physical and biological effects, that goes along with the elevational change. As noted in Chapter 1, on average, air and soil temperatures decrease by about 3 degrees for every 1,000-foot increase in elevation in the Northeast's mountains. Along with this decrease, annual precipitation increases about 8 inches and both factors have a significant influence on tree growth.

The most obvious effect of lower temperatures is that chemical and biological reaction rates are reduced, slowing all life processes, even for organisms adapted to growing in cold places. Plants sometimes show a remarkable ability to adjust to temperature changes—balsam fir at high elevation, for example, carries out photosynthesis more efficiently at low temperatures than it does in the valleys. But by and large, the rates of photosynthesis and conversion of carbohydrates into new tissues are much reduced at high elevations. Low temperatures also have an important influence on the development of soils at high elevation. Slower chemical reactions mean reduced breakdown of rock and slower release of mineral nutrients. And reduced microbial activity in the colder soils means slower decomposition and nutrient turnover, creating a bottleneck in the circulation of materials within the forest ecosystem. Adding to these effects, the increased precipitation, while contributing some nutrients to the soil, also leaches the soil of its more soluble elements and carries them down into the lower forests, leaving the upper slopes nutrient poor. At higher elevations, then, is where the evergreen advantage (page 42) comes into play again.

The transition from hardwood to conifer forest is a surprisingly abrupt one. By 3,000 feet the only remnants of the hardwood forest are an occasional yellow birch and a few understory herbs and shrubs—such as wood sorrel, shining club moss, clintonia, and hobblebush—that make it through the transition. Balsam fir increases in numbers and the trees grow thickly. We are now in the subalpine spruce-fir zone.

These subalpine forests are built on an old felsenmeer ("sea of rock") substrate, frost-shattered rock left over from a period of intense cold following retreat of the mountain glaciers. Water that seeped into the cracks of the freshly exposed bedrock froze, expanded, and with a force approaching 20 tons per square inch wedged the rock apart, breaking it into a rubble of sharp, angular fragments very different from the smoothly rounded boulders and cobbles left in the lowlands. On this rock pile the northern Appalachians' subalpine forests perch with their roots probing among the pockets and crevices for a grip. And sometimes their grip is only tentative. When the wind blows hard you can often feel the ground move underfoot as trees sway and roots are wrenched and scraped and broken. In places, the trees are tossed randomly about, one across another, under high winds or heavy snow loads; and in this cold forest where decomposition is so slow, they lie so for decades, a deterrent to even the most determined off-trail hikers.

Covering this rocky substrate is a thick forest floor of organic matter. Spruce and fir seem to have little problem regenerating here; in places they

## Nonconformists in the Boreal Forest

AS THE DECIDUOUS hardwood trees extend their ranges farther north or higher into the mountains, they experience still shorter growing seasons, eventually reaching their limits where the tree can produce only enough photosynthate during the summer to cover its year-round maintenance needs. From this point on, colonization is a losing proposition and the hardwoods give way to the more conservative conifers. The exceptions are always noteworthy, and one has to marvel at the ability of paper birch and aspen to grow all the way to the arctic treeline. These trees are competing against an evergreen strategy that is indisputably successful throughout the far northern forest, and it's fun to speculate about how they manage it.

One possibility is that limited photosynthetic activity in bark tissues supplements the photosynthesis in the leaves. It would be no surprise to find substantial amounts of chlorophyll in the very green bark of aspen, but it so happens that paper birch also has a good amount of chlorophyll in its inner bark, as do many other deciduous species. And some photosynthesis has been measured in leafless twigs of a number of different species immediately after a thaw in midwinter. It is tempting to suggest that aspen and birch survive in the far north by complementing stores from their efficient summer leaves with at least occasional bark photosynthesis during the warmer days of winter. The same may also be true of tamarack, the only deciduous conifer found in the North Woods. While bark photosynthesis may account for only a small percentage of a tree's overall annual carbohydrate gains, any opportunity to offset the continual drain of energy reserves that occurs through respiration during the winter would seem to be of adaptive value.

---

grow so densely that scarcely any light reaches the ground beneath them. If there is any ground cover at all it is likely to be a carpet of haircap moss and a miniature understory of wood sorrel mixed with goldthread, bunchberry, and the single leaves of sterile Canada mayflower—all evergreen herbs. If the soil is wet, sphagnum moss may provide the only ground cover. Where there is a little more light, spinulose wood fern grows thickly along with wood asters and clintonia. And along the trailside or where a tree has been uprooted to expose mineral soil, we find a variety of plants typical of the higher elevations—currant, mountain ash, paper birch—but elsewhere, late-lying snow and frequent June frosts limit most other plant species.

As plant productivity (the total amount of energy captured through photosynthesis) and species diversity decline, so too does the animal community dwindle. Though the forests of our higher mountains are dominated by the same spruce and fir as in our lowlands, the flow of energy through the subalpine ecosystem is considerably reduced and the number of mammals and birds that can be supported here diminishes accordingly. The smaller mammals—deer mice, red-backed voles, squirrels, snowshoe hares, and the occasional porcupine, along with their predators—can still make a living, although in reduced numbers, but the larger mammals are mostly transient now. No mammal species are unique to the subalpine forests.

Though avian diversity is similarly diminished, a number of birds breed in our subalpine forests. One of the most familiar, the white-throated sparrow, graces the stunted spruce and fir all summer with its thin, high-pitched song, *Oh sweet Canada, Canada, Canada*. Perhaps the most noteworthy of the migrants, however, are the blackpoll warbler and Bicknell's thrush. The blackpoll warbler is a bird of exceptional capability. This is the champion distance flyer of all the warblers, with some individuals covering the longest migratory route of all but three or four migrants in the western hemisphere. The blackpoll warbler ranges across the entire North American boreal forest, from northern New England and the Maritime Provinces to the coast of Alaska. When it migrates south for winter, the entire breeding population funnels eastward across the continent to southeastern Canada and New England before departing on a non-stop, trans-Atlantic route to South America, to winter as far south as Brazil and northern Argentina. This translates into a round-trip of several thousand miles on average—for a 4-inch bird weighing only half an ounce! And if that were not impressive enough, ornithologists tell us that individual blackpolls, at the end of their journey, often return to the same tree in their breeding grounds for nesting!

From a conservation standpoint, the most notable of our migrants is unquestionably the Bicknell's thrush. This thrush, long thought to be a variant of the gray-cheeked thrush, was not identified as a separate species until 1995. Difficult to observe in the field for its secretive habits, and equally difficult to distinguish by sight from the gray-cheeked thrush, Bicknell's thrush is, nonetheless, distinctive in hand as being smaller than its look-alike, with subtle differences in plumage, song, range, and now DNA

## Bicknell's Thrush

THE FIRST RECORDED specimen of a Bicknell's thrush was shot in 1881 by an amateur ornithologist roaming the Catskill Mountains of New York. An astute birder, Eugene Bicknell was perplexed by what he had just collected, so he sent his specimen to an expert at the American Museum of Natural History for identification. There the bird was designated as a new subspecies of gray-cheeked thrush, a bird known from higher elevations in northern New England and eastern Canada, and was given the name Bicknell's thrush.

For the next 100 years, Bicknell's thrush was all but forgotten. Brief interest in it in the 1930s, as the subject of a doctoral dissertation, supported its listing as a subspecies of gray-cheeked thrush, and there it remained until more than half a century later when Henri Ouellet of the National Museum of Natural Sciences in Ottawa got interested. His systematic study subsequently showed several important differences between Bicknell's and gray-cheeked thrushes. Bicknell's thrush was not only smaller, as Ouellet's predecessors had noticed, with differences in coloration of the lower mandible and upper tail feathers, but more importantly, neither its summer nor winter range overlapped that of the gray-cheeked thrush. (The latter breeds farther north in Canada and winters in South America.) In addition, the calls and songs of the two birds differ. In limited trials, Dr. Ouellet found that the Bicknell's thrush did not respond to songs of the gray-cheeked thrush. Then it was discovered that genetic markers had diverged significantly between the two birds, and the case was clinched. Bicknell's thrush was elevated to a new species by the American Ornithological Union in 1995.

Almost immediately, Bicknell's thrush became the subject of intense monitoring. Its world population is currently estimated at no more than 50,000, 90 percent of which winter on one island—Hispaniola—in the Caribbean. Given its highly specific and widely scattered breeding habitat in the subalpine forests of northeastern North America, coupled with its narrow geographic distribution at both ends of its migratory route, Bicknell's thrush may be particularly vulnerable to environmental change in the future.

analysis (see "Bicknell's Thrush" on page 97). Breeding solely in our subalpine forests, in the stunted spruce and fir of isolated mountain tops throughout our region (including small populations in the Catskills and in the Maritime Provinces), Bicknell's thrush is a jewel in the cloud forest, its flute-like vocalizations as ethereal and mysterious as the bird itself.

## Dealing with Disturbance

As we have already seen, community composition changes dramatically with disturbance, and disturbance is an important aspect of the northern Appalachians' subalpine forest ecosystems. We previously noted that wind throw is common on these rocky soils, and in a moment we will see how wind exposure leads to another form of cyclic dieback that periodically opens up the forest. But even the deep snow cover accumulating on the higher slopes helps shape these subalpine forests. The slow but inexorable creep of snow downhill under its own weight puts constant pressure on the trees, causing them to grow asymmetrically, with "pistol butt" bases arching upward from the sloping ground. And where slopes are especially steep, the snowpack periodically slips, sending an avalanche roaring down the mountainside, a wide swath of broken trees in its wake. In some of the steep-sided ravines on the leeward sides of ridges in the White Mountains, like Tuckerman and Huntington ravines on Mount Washington, avalanches occur repeatedly along the same course, their tracks marked by the dense growth of mountain alder and shrubby paper birch that lie pressed to the ground under the weight of snow during much of the year. Landslides, too, occasionally open a swath through the subalpine forest, allowing colonization of the soil by species not normally represented in the closed spruce-fir stand.

In many of the high-elevation fir forests of the northern Appalachians we find a particularly interesting phenomenon of cyclic disturbance and rejuvenation that may help explain how these stands came to be nearly pure fir in the first place. Punctuating the dark green ridges of the Adirondack High Peaks region and the northern White Mountains (and to a much lesser extent the Green Mountains) are numerous silvery, often crescent-shaped bands of dying trees. These bands are found on the more wind-exposed slopes and are usually oriented in the same direction, often in rows, as if controlled by some underlying structure. Many of our hiking trails intersect these dieback areas, and when we walk through them we often pass them off as random blowdown. But they result from a much more dynamic process, and when we look closely at these areas we notice that in fact the trees are standing dead, having died on their feet long before their bare trunks were to be toppled by the wind.

These dieback zones are part of a "fir wave," and so far as is known, they occur in just two parts of the world—the northern Appalachian Mountain chain and the mountains of Japan (see Figure 14). Fir waves are moving bands of death and regeneration that advance systematically through mature forest stands at a rate of 3 to 10 feet per year. Nearly all trees in the path of these waves succumb, while fir, almost exclusively, regenerates in their wake. This configuration gives the forest a wavelike profile: Just behind the advancing dieback zone tree height abruptly decreases, but with greater distance from the dieback, trees become progressively older and taller, until the wave "crests" at another dieback zone with sapling regeneration behind it. The distance between two successive wave fronts varies with the rate of movement and the age of the forest stand, but it averages around 200 feet, with a repeat time of 60 to 70 years. These waves can move upslope or downslope, but they always

**FIGURE 14** "Fir waves" are moving bands of dying trees that advance uphill into a mature stand. Note that trees along the leading edge are standing dead, not simply wind-thrown. Such cyclic disturbance is common in the high-elevation fir forests of the northern Appalachians.

progress in the direction of the prevailing wind, and the end of the wave always comes when it passes over the crest of a ridge.

The death of trees occurs fairly rapidly in a fir wave and results from an accumulation of stresses over time. Forest stands in wave-prone areas are basically even aged—the trees all spring up together when the overstory opens up. While the trees are saplings, growing conditions are not too bad. The young trees are reasonably sheltered and have ample moisture available, and as light floods the forest floor they grow vigorously. But with stand densities sometimes exceeding 5,000 trees per acre, the competition for scarce resources soon becomes intense. Reaching for sunlight under increasingly crowded conditions, the trees grow lean, lower branches get shaded out, and with time, the amount of foliage relative to the increasing mass of the tree diminishes. The trees must compete for everything now, and as they race for light they grow with virtually no taper at all, eventually to a height of 25 or 30 feet. As the trees outgrow their shelter close to the ground, they become precariously balanced on the thin mantle of soil, and they lean on each other for support as they increasingly suffer mechanical stresses from wind exposure.

When the trees were young and vigorous, they produced photosynthate in excess of their maintenance needs and had surplus energy reserves to deal with problems of mechanical injury, like tissue repair and replacement. But when the trees are larger and have more living tissue in roots, trunk, and crown to provide for, their respiration costs are far greater, and the tree is no longer able to produce photosynthate in excess of what is needed for maintenance. The trees also have reached a height where they suffer greater pressure from the wind and from heavy accumulations of rime ice that collects as cold clouds sweep across the mountain slopes (see "Rime Ice" on page 101). The weather-beaten trees begin to lose productive foliage and soon are barely breaking even in terms of meeting their needs. If a single tree goes down now and opens up a small gap in the canopy, the force of the wind at the exposed canopy edge increases and the trees situated along the downwind side of the gap lose still more foliage. The trees begin to sway more in the wind, rocking back and forth on the shallow substrate, and their root systems suffer considerable abrasive damage, adding to their problems. Fungi in the soil that normally make their living by decomposing dead organic matter

## Rime Ice

THE WINDS THAT sculpture trees at high elevations display an element of artistry that often rewards those who make a summit climb in subfreezing conditions. Few of nature's weather tricks are as impressive as the feather work of rime ice on trees and rocks that protrude into the cloud stream on a cold day.

Rime ice forms when clouds, swept by high winds across the mountainside in cold weather, leave frozen droplets on anything exposed. The water droplets in the cloud are very small, and because their surface tension is so high, they resist freezing and remain liquid at temperatures well below the freezing point of water—even down to minus 40 degrees. But this "super-cooled" state is a very tenuous one, and impact with any cold object results in instantaneous crystallization of the water droplet. As the cloud sweeps past a tree, ice builds up on the windward side of every branch and every needle, growing in thickness as one tiny cloud droplet after another hits and freezes. If the wind is very strong and steady from one direction, ice will build outward in thin feathery vanes pointing into the wind and creating an ice sculpture of exquisite detail.

For all its intricate beauty, though, rime ice can wreak havoc on an evergreen conifer. As winds shift, the ice-encrusted foliage of the conifer is sent sailing away, and along with it much of the promise of another growing season. In subalpine fir forests, up to one-fifth of the foliage of trees exposed to wind at the edge of canopy gaps may come down during the winter as a result of this ice loading—a loss from which some trees never recover.

move into the wounded root tissues and begin to parasitize the tree, tapping it for carbohydrates and placing still more demand on limited photosynthetic reserves. The tree responds to this injury by taking the affected root out of service but often over-corrects, closing off more root tissue than was actually damaged. Now the tree is under duress at both ends, losing foliage and roots at an accelerated pace, and in an environment where growing conditions may be marginal to begin with, the loss is just too great. The tree eventually dies by attrition. The opening in the canopy grows larger, the process of death is repeated along the exposed edge, and a fir wave is born.

To the individual tree the result is, of course, disastrous. To the aging forest as a whole, however, the process has a more positive effect. Nutrients that have been tied up for decades in the wood of the tree are released again, sunlight reaches the understory once more, and for a while the forest will be young and vigorous. We see these fir waves now as an important mechanism in the cyclic renewal of the Northeast's subalpine forests, which are too moist for fires and too cold for insect outbreaks that would otherwise periodically rejuvenate an aging forest.

## The Limits to Tree Growth

A few years ago I happened to be up on Franconia Ridge in the White Mountains when a trail crew from the Appalachian Mountain Club was reconstructing parts of the Appalachian Trail. As I watched a crew member digging a trench across the trail for a water bar, I remember pondering how deep the mineral soil was at that particular spot. I wondered then why the soil did not support the growth of trees rather than the healthy sedge turf of its alpine lawn. Just 50 feet away and not 10 feet lower in elevation, the impenetrable thickets of balsam fir and black spruce ended abruptly, and the low-growing herbaceous sedges and rushes had taken over from there (see Figure 15). As part of my doctoral studies, I had spent three winters on Mount Washington researching similar questions about the limits to tree growth, yet here I was still asking why. I knew a few things now that were *not* limiting forest advance at that elevation, but I still had many questions.

The treeline, the edge of the forest as a physiognomic or ecological unit, forms one of the most abrupt and conspicuous boundaries between two different vegetation types to be found anywhere on earth. Crossing the treeline

**FIGURE 15** This small island of krummholz is hanging on tenuously, just above the alpine treeline. Many interacting forces keep the forest as a whole from advancing into the tundra.

takes you from an environment influenced significantly by biological processes, where the growing climate is modified by the trees themselves, to one in which physical forces dominate—where the plants have very little modifying effect on their environment. And few species, plant or animal, regularly inhabit both sides of the treeline. Even human cultures have evolved separately on one side or the other; in the far north, the arctic treeline forms a distinct boundary between Eskimo cultures adapted to life in the open tundra and woodland Indian cultures adapted to life in the boreal forest. So it is understandable that trying to explain the causes and fluctuations in treelines over time has attracted the attention of many researchers—climatologists, geographers, and ecologists alike. What makes generalizations about the cause of treelines difficult is that, somewhere in the world, there is a good case in support of almost any hypothesis that has ever been presented.

In considering the particular treeline situation in the northern Appalachians, let's start with the underlying assumption that the forest limit in these mountains is climatically controlled rather than influenced by human activity. This may seem so obvious as to need no mention, but elsewhere in the world human influences have much to do with the nature and position of the treeline, especially where fuel-wood gathering and the grazing of livestock at high elevations are important occupations. Intriguing place names for some of the Northeast's alpine areas, like the Cow Pasture in the alpine zone on Mount Washington, suggest the possibility of local grazing sometime in the past, but documentation of this kind of activity in the high mountains of the northern Appalachians is lacking. And while these mountains have, as we have seen, a long history of logging, it is not likely that this activity has left any impression on the present treeline. Pulpwood cutting has occurred at one time or another high into the forests of nearly every mountainside, but logging of the marginal subalpine forests has never been commercially feasible.

It doesn't appear, either, that tree growth is limited by the absence of suitable substrate at high elevations. While soils of the alpine zone are generally shallow (my earlier recollection notwithstanding) and low in essential nutrients, these same soils support substantial forest growth at lower elevations, and there is no abrupt change above the treeline in either the nature of these soils or their depth. It seems reasonable, therefore, to assume that the present position and form of the treeline in this region is controlled by some form of interaction between trees and the climate—a likelihood suggested by the stunted, gnarled, and flagged (one-sided) form of the trees themselves.

The influence of climate on forest development is multifaceted, as we have already noted, and limitations at the forest edge may involve restrictions at any phase in a tree's growth and development. One of the more widely accepted notions about the cause of treeline is that trees at the forest edge commonly suffer death by desiccation. This is assumed to be a particularly acute problem during winter, when the water lost from foliage exposed to the sun and wind cannot be replaced because the soil is frozen. In some treeline areas of the world, this condition is no doubt a severe limitation. Where excessive winter water loss is a problem, it is usually tied to incomplete maturation of needles, in particular of their protective waxy cuticle, due to a short, cool growing season. But winter desiccation does not seem to be much of a problem in the northern Appalachians, partly because wind, surprisingly enough, is not the true culprit when it comes to water loss from a dormant tree. The real problem arises when foliage exposed to intense solar radiation above the snowpack, while sheltered from the wind, heats as much as 25 or 30 degrees above air temperature. Heating the leaf drives water out of it, and if the exposed foliage is thawed while the rest of the tree remains frozen, the result is invariably damaging water loss. But this does not happen under cloud cover or when the wind is blowing, two conditions that seem to prevail throughout the winter at the treeline in the Northeast. When a tree is exposed to strong sunlight above the snow cover, even a slight increase in wind dissipates excess heat and reduces, rather than increases, water loss.

This is not to suggest that wind isn't a problem at the treeline, however. To the contrary, whatever ultimately causes the death of upright shoots is almost certainly related to wind exposure. A tree sheltered in the lee of a rock will usually do very well until it outgrows its protection, and then, if the leader survives at all, its branches become strongly flagged to one side as the various actions of the wind shape the tree. Often we see balsam fir and red spruce at the treeline producing multiple upright leaders that repeatedly die back while the lateral branches close to the ground fare much better, producing a dense cluster of basal foliage. Sometimes the tree is so perfectly trimmed as to show very graphically the flow of wind over a protective ridge or large rock. A distinction should be made here, though, between wind "training," where branches subjected to a steady force on the windward side are trained to grow around to the leeward side, and storm "pruning," where branches on the windward side suffer death by one cause or another and are eventually broken off in high winds. Most flagging at the treeline results from the latter.

A common form of wind damage in the northern Appalachians is abrasion from wind-carried ice particles. Like sand blowing across a beach dune, ice grains whipping over the snowpack have tremendous abrasive power on the relatively soft tissues of exposed trees. Bark on the windward sides of exposed trunks is sometimes abraded right to the wood, and within that zone of maximum transport just above the surface of the snow, foliage may be stripped away entirely. And once needles are broken off, desiccating water loss often follows.

Apart from the obvious physical damage, this loss of photosynthetic tissue is critical under marginal growing conditions, as we saw in fir waves

**FIGURE 16** Ice particles whipped by high winds on Mount Washington strip branches of foliage during winter. The growth of surviving buds may eventually elevate the crown above the zone of maximum abrasion, producing a "mop head" of foliage.

at slightly lower elevations. These needles begin photosynthesis early in the spring, building up reserve energy that contributes substantially to the tree's growth before new needles begin to pay back their own costs, and the loss of these overwintering needles may never be recovered. If the terminal buds somehow survive this peril each winter, and if summer growing conditions are favorable, the tree may eventually reach above the zone of abrasion to maintain a "mop head" of foliage at the top of a bare trunk, a growth habit known as broomsticking (see Figure 16). But the struggle for a tenuous

**FIGURE 17** Black spruce shows remarkable genetic flexibility, growing entirely prostrate above treeline. Spreading by means of adventitious roots, the "tree" exploits a warmer microclimate and completely avoids the problems of ice blast in winter.

position is difficult; success in this case often brings on other problems like increased encrustation by rime ice, which is likely to break off in the wind, taking foliage with it.

The most successful tree species at the treeline is the prostrate mat form of black spruce (see Figure 17). This species has the genetic flexibility to change its growth habit according to the demands of its environment, and can spread by means of adventitious roots that develop from branches. Thus the black spruce grows in a mat, without ever attempting to produce an upright leader. The mats show little evidence of physical damage, as they remain protected under the snowpack during most of the winter. But by growing along the ground instead of upright, these trees are also exploiting a much warmer microclimate, which highlights another important aspect of wind exposure—its effect on plant temperatures during the summer. When the snow cover is gone, both the ground and the plant foliage provide a dark surface that absorbs incoming solar radiation and heats up, warming the air close to the ground. While wind might easily dissipate this heat, wind speed drops off sharply near the ground, so the closer the plant grows to the ground, the warmer it is—an obvious advantage during the growing season. Thus "protection," as we have used the word, may mean freedom from physical abuse, or it may mean a more favorable thermal environment through reduction of wind speed. In most cases it is likely a combination of the two.

Survival and growth are not the only considerations at any treeline. If the forest is to maintain itself or advance into the tundra, successful reproduction is also required. Whether or not this poses a serious limitation at the treeline in the Northeast is difficult to say with certainty. Black spruce at the treeline produces infrequent cone crops, and the seeds often are incompletely developed. But a tree that produces a successful seed crop only once or twice in a century can establish enough seedlings to keep a stand going. Black spruce also reproduces vegetatively, as was noted earlier. Balsam fir, on the other hand, produces cone crops more frequently, and is at least occasionally successful in establishing seedlings at the treeline. On Mount Washington, for instance, a winter road above the treeline is used now and again by maintenance crews driving tracked vehicles, and here, where the normal cover of tundra vegetation is very sparse, the edges of the road are sometimes crowded with numerous healthy fir seedlings. So it appears fir can reproduce at the treeline under favorable site conditions, although opportunities for seedlings to establish themselves amid the undisturbed tundra vegetation are limited.

When we analyze the growth rings of trees at the forest limit in the northern Appalachians, we find that, however narrow the rings might be, the trees usually manage to add wood every year. This may be taken as evidence that the trees are producing enough photosynthate to satisfy their basic needs. The allocation of carbohydrate among the various tissues and growth functions of a tree is prioritized, and wood is generally lowest on the list, so that if there

**FIGURE 18** Time-lapse photographs of a balsam fir at treeline on Mount Washington. Four years after the photo at left (a) was taken, the tree has made little progress (b). Summertime gains are repeatedly offset by winter losses, with the tree barely breaking even in the long term.

is not enough carbohydrate to go around, wood production is dropped. A tree might need to produce wood for competitive reasons, but no physiological reasons make it necessary every year. For example, when growing under severe drought stress, trees in the Southwest may fail to produce wood during many growing seasons but still live on for centuries. So while growth is very much reduced at the treeline, it is apparently sufficient for the tree to maintain itself in the absence of other physiological constraints.

The problem here, though, seems to be too little "profit margin" during the summer to cover wintertime losses. Abrasive damage by wind-carried ice particles and rime-ice encrustation can remove as much foliage from branches exposed above the snowpack as was produced the previous year (see Figures 18a and 18b). Maintaining such a precarious balance between leaf gains and losses in this environment will never suffice. As production of woody tissues continues, respiration requirements may increase until a compensation point is reached and the annual carbohydrate budget of the tree is no longer balanced. Some part of the tree will then die. So the relatively low timberline in the northern Appalachians seems best explained in terms of low photosynthetic production coupled with heavy annual loss of leaf and shoot tissues owing to high winds.

## LAND ABOVE THE TREES

While trees at the forest limit may have trouble balancing their carbon budgets, the low-growing shrubs and herbs in the tundra beyond seem to have found the secret. In this most limiting of mountain environments, miniaturization appears to be the answer. Dwarf willows, birches, and heath shrubs may grow upright in the protected hollows among rocks; but elsewhere they sprawl, like the prostrate black spruce at the treeline, flat on the ground seeking a warmer microclimate, that thin protective zone where the wind does not hit as hard and the air is warmed by the soil's absorption of solar radiation (see Figure 19). Other plants do the same. The mountain sandwort

**FIGURE 19** Like the prostrate black spruce at treeline, this dwarf willow in the alpine tundra is genetically "programmed" to grow prostrate along the ground, where it takes advantage of the sun's warmth absorbed by soil and rock.

that often lines trails above the treeline grows in small tufts barely an inch in height, with narrow leaves loosely interwoven that trap the precious warmth at ground level. Diapensia grows in such a compact "cushion" that it creates its own self-sustaining microenvironment. Its tightly packed leaves are almost impervious to the wind, and the organic soil that accumulates beneath its dark, absorbing foliage may be several degrees warmer than the surrounding air. Thus the common theme in the alpine tundra is staying small and low to the ground to make the most of the advantages gained by absorbing sunlight. Here permanency is no longer a matter of adding support tissue every year to hold the plant up, for this game is won not by mechanical strength but by subtle, often invisible strategies—internal physiological adjustments to match the outward physical modifications. And the small size of these plants keeps maintenance needs to a minimum, helping substantially to balance the carbohydrate budget of each plant in an energy-deficient environment.

That such morphological characteristics in alpine vegetation have emerged so universally through genetic trial and error is not surprising in light of the nature of alpine environments everywhere. To be sure, calm days occur on the high summits when the brilliance of the sun is unmatched anywhere else, and they too are part of the weather complex to which alpine plants must remain sensitive. But the frequent summit visitor knows too well that the opposite extreme is more often the case: The Northeast's alpine areas are frequently shrouded in clouds, pummeled for days at a time by high winds, and subjected to snow and freezing temperatures during any month of the growing season. Consider for a minute that on Mount Washington in New Hampshire, cloud cover obscures the summit 55 percent of the time; wind speed averages 35 miles per hour day and night, with hurricane-force winds of 74 miles per hour or greater occurring during every month of the year; and the highest temperature ever recorded at the Mount Washington Observatory is only 72 degrees.

Mount Washington is the extreme, of course, but weather records collected at other high-elevation stations like Mount Mansfield in Vermont and Whiteface Mountain in the Adirondacks tell the same story: Conditions in the alpine zone are cold and windy throughout the growing season. These are the conditions to which plants must adapt. Survival during winter is not enough, for alpine plants must also be able to grow and reproduce at the low temperatures of summer, and they are superbly adapted to doing so.

In an environment dominated by physical forces, where the plants themselves exert little influence on growing conditions, we might expect to see a fairly homogeneous vegetation cover—a single alpine community adapted to a common set of environmental constraints. But such is not the case, for even here we find plants varying in their tolerances, with seemingly small differences in topography and microclimate making a big difference in the distribution of species. The highland rush, a number of different sedges, and the heath shrubs dominate alpine vegetation, and they differ from one another in their response to temperature, soil moisture, and tolerance of late-lying snow cover. Thus they form different communities recognizable by the relative proportions of each species. On the coldest slopes, especially north- and west-facing exposures with frequent fog and high soil moisture, we find sedge meadows dominating (see Figure 20). This community is characterized by the

**FIGURE 20** In the upper reaches of the alpine zone, where slopes are steeped in cloud moisture and the organic soils are continuously wet, sedge meadows form the dominant community type. Here, Bigelow's sedge is the most abundant plant species.

abundance of Bigelow's sedge, which produces shoots from underground stems and often forms a dense turf over the rocky substrate. As we move downslope, highland rush and various heath shrubs intermix in an association called (logically) the sedge-heath-rush community. Where drainage is better and snow melts early, the sedge may drop out and the others take over. The heath-rush community so formed is often found on south- and east-facing exposures and is dominated by mountain cranberry, alpine bilberry, and, of course, the highland rush. Still further downslope, usually just above the treeline or in protected places where the snow cover is deep but not long lasting, the rush disappears and the heath shrubs dominate. Labrador tea and black crowberry are often prominent in this community, along with the other heath shrubs common to the alpine zone.

Two other easily recognizable communities occupy the extremes of snow-cover conditions. Some of the tallest plants to be found in the alpine zone make up the snowbank community. Species like Indian poke (also known as false hellebore), hairgrass, and Cutler's goldenrod are found where the snow lies deep and stays long but where late snowmelt provides ample water to support their rapid growth. These snowbank species are almost always found on the lee sides of mountain ridges, and because of the protection that such locations afford, herbs from the lower forests sometimes make it into this community. At the opposite end of the spectrum, the diapensia community, consisting primarily of that species, alpine azalea, and Lapland rosebay, flourishes under what would seem the greatest difficulty of all—the most windswept exposures to be found anywhere in the alpine zone. There, where protective snows are continually blown clear, diapensia sometimes persists alone (see Figure 21). Few other species compete successfully under these conditions.

The plants of these alpine communities display many different adaptations, some of which have evolved along parallel lines in very different life forms. The nonvascular lichens and mosses, for example, are very successful in the alpine zone partly because they are able to maintain photosynthetic production at very low temperatures. Some, in fact, continue photosynthetic activity into the winter, having the ability during periods of brief thaw to absorb meltwater directly into their photosynthetic tissues. But the dwarf woody shrubs, whether deciduous or evergreen, are

**FIGURE 21** On the most windswept ridges of the high alpine zone, diapensia flourishes, creating its own life-support system beneath a tightly packed envelope of drought-resistant foliage. Where the ground is blown free of snow most of the winter, few other plants can compete successfully.

equally successful in their respective niches. So, too, are the cushion plants, the leafy herbs, and the sedges. The only "rule" that is nearly universal in alpine environments is that the plants, regardless of life form, be perennials. The alpine tundra is no place for annuals—plants that in a single growing season must germinate from seed, grow to maturity, flower, and produce more viable seed to perpetuate the species. The growing season is much too compressed for this. While there are a few interesting exceptions in other alpine areas of the world (and their success makes them fascinating objects of study), the alpine communities in the Northeast, as elsewhere, are dominated by perennials.

These perennials assure their own permanence in ways more reliable than through seed production alone. The majority of the vascular plants invest heavily in roots and rhizomes (underground stems), often producing two to ten times as much mass below ground as above. These belowground organs serve as carbohydrate storage centers that support growth early in the following summer, and it is from them that many plants produce vegetative offshoots—a common habit in the alpine zone and a hedge against the high risk of seed failure. The advantage of vegetative reproduction is a much greater probability of success—a sure start and a genetic makeup identical to the parent's, already proven in an environment that selects rigorously against the unfit. But vegetative reproduction is a mixed promise. In some respects, the progeny may be too reliant on the parent. The offspring must depend on parental resources for early development; they are restricted to the parent's site; and perhaps most importantly, they lack the genetic flexibility to adjust to changing environmental conditions. Vegetative reproduction is an ideal way to preserve a genetic makeup that has proved successful, because it prevents the introduction of less favorable genetic traits through cross-fertilization. However, if the environment changes—for instance, if the climate slowly warms or cools or annual precipitation changes in amount or seasonal distribution—then the species may not be able to readapt. Vegetative reproduction, with the constraints of a fixed genetic character, may be an evolutionary dead end.

However, few alpine plants rely on vegetative reproduction alone. Many of these plants, even the species noted for their copious production of vegetative offshoots and turf-forming ability, sometimes flower prolifically and during a good seed year may produce hundreds of seeds. A patch of mountain

**CUTLER'S GOLDENROD *(Solidago cutleri)*** A dwarf goldenrod of alpine summits, standing 2 to 10 inches tall. Flowers in terminal clusters with leaves mostly in a basal rosette. Named for eighteenth century minister and natural historian Manasseh Cutler, who made early estimates of elevations in the White Mountains. Blooms in late summer.

**BLACK CROWBERRY *(Empetrum nigrum)*** Ground-hugging evergreen, with leaves closely packed; shaped like small fir needles. Flowers, small and inconspicuous, located in leaf axils, giving rise to large purplish berries that turn black with age. Fruits persistent into winter; taste best after first frost.

**ALPINE BILLBERRY *(Vaccinium uliginosum)*** Larval host for the heath sulfur butterfly. Distinctly rounded leaves with net-like veins distinguish this from other heath shrubs. Recent studies have shown flavinoid pigments in the fruits to have high antioxidative activity.

**MOUNTAIN CRANBERRY
(Vaccinium vitis-idaea)** Species
name refers to the grape of
Mount Ida in Greek mythology.
A low-growing evergreen shrub,
circumpolar in distribution.
Known as lingonberry in northern
Europe. Fruit tart, improving after
freezing. Popular for preserves
or syrup; also high in antioxidants.

**ALPINE AZALEA (Loiseleuria
procumbens)** Dense, mat-forming
shrub with leaves and flowers
scarcely more than one-eighth of
an inch in length. Evergreen leaves
are leathery, rolled under at the
margins, with dense hairs beneath.
Circumpolar in distribution, found in
high mountains of northern North
America and Eurasia.

**LAPLAND ROSEBAY
(Rhododendron lapponicum)** Latin
name means "rose tree." A miniature
rhododendron shrub, often no more
than 2 inches high, rarely reaching 12
inches. One of the earliest blooming
alpine plants, with flowers opening
before new leaves are developed.

**MOUNTAIN SANDWORT**
*(Minuartia groenlandicum)* Formerly placed in genus Arenaria, sometimes referred to as a stitchwort. Small plant, commonly growing in tufts. One of few alpine plants that could be considered a true pioneer species on disturbed soils.

**THREE-TOOTHED CINQUEFOIL**
*(Sibbaldiopsis tridentata)* Formerly placed in genus Potentilla, named for its distinctive leaf tip. Stems sprawling, woody at the base, non-woody and light green toward the tips. Evergreen leaves often turn dark red in autumn. Frequently found in disturbed alpine areas due to persistence of woody belowground parts.

**DIAPENSIA** *(Diapensia lapponica)*
A plant of windswept alpine ridges. Grows in dense "cushions" with tightly packed leaves that trap soil and heat, creating a self-supporting microclimate. Larval host for the arctic blue butterfly.

### MOUNTAIN HEATH
*(Phyllodoce caerulea)* Shrub less than 6 inches tall. Flowers urn-shaped; leaves tightly rolled at margins, resembling flattened needles. A circumpolar species widely distributed across Canada, Greenland, and Eurasia, persisting in the U.S. only in Alaska and the alpine summits of New England. Named for the sea nymph in Greek mythology, but allusion is obscure.

### INDIAN POKE
*(Veratrum viride)* One of few lower-elevation plants making it into the alpine zone. Found in protected areas where snow accumulates and provides abundant meltwater during growing season. Unlike most alpine plants, leaves are large and broad; many reach 2 feet in height. All parts contain steroidal alkaloids and are toxic.

### ALPINE BISTORT
*(Polygonum vivaparum)* Circumpolar species of arctic and alpine habitats but uncommon now in the Northeast, possibly extirpated in Vermont. Species name refers to reproduction by bulbils (small bulbs) attached to stem below flowers, sometimes initiating growth before falling from plant. Rarely produces viable seeds, rendering it vulnerable to environmental change.

## Lichens

Nothing contributes as much to the far-north feeling in our spruce-fir forests as do the lichens that drape the branches and trunks of weathered conifers. Lichens, in fact, exemplify plant adaptation to the rigors of the boreal forest and the tundra beyond. These lichens are not parasitic organisms relying on their host for sustenance; rather they are free-living plants using the tree solely for mechanical support and as a means to obtain more sunlight than is available on the forest floor.

Lichens are actually composed of two distinctly different plant forms, an alga and a fungus, growing together where neither is able to succeed alone. The fungal partner is basically a decomposer organism. It produces no chlorophyll and, when not associated with algae, obtains its energy from the breakdown of dead organic matter. In the lichen association, however, the fungus derives considerable benefit by harboring photosynthetic algal cells that transfer sugars from their own chlorophyllous tissues to the fungus. From this vantage point, the fungus seems to benefit most from the association. It actually regulates, even suppresses, the growth of the algal cells in a kind of controlled parasitism. The relationship is not entirely one-sided, however, as the algal cells benefit both from the mechanical protection provided by the fungal body and from the nutrients absorbed by fungal hyphae (the equivalent of roots). For this reason, lichens are usually cited as an example of true symbiosis.

The question of whether or not one partner benefits more than the other in this relationship is only academic, for the combination of life forms in a single organism is remarkably successful under the harshest of conditions. Lichens are resistant to extreme low temperatures and are able in some cases to photosynthesize at below-freezing temperatures. They can withstand extended droughts (lichens are common in hot deserts as well as polar environments) and then "revive" instantly by absorbing water directly into their photosynthetic tissues. And they are able to extract nutrients where there is no soil at all, chemically etching the surface of bare rock for scarce minerals or straining water as it drips down the branches of a tree. Lichens are indeed the foremost pioneers of the plant world, but most have little resistance to the pollutants of our technological world, especially sulfur dioxide, and some species have disappeared entirely from areas affected by even low-level industrial emissions.

sandwort no larger than what your wool hat might cover can yield up to 2,000 seeds in a growing season. Diapensia, highland rush, and many other herbs and shrubs are also capable of high seed production. The seeds in these cases are generally viable and often lack any built-in dormancy mechanism, so that they germinate readily as soon as soil temperatures are right for the particular species.

The problems of successful sexual (flowering) reproduction, however, lie not with seed production, but with seed dispersal and seedling establishment. Although it seems counterintuitive, the high winds of the alpine zone are not especially effective in blowing seeds around. The plants are, after all, of very low stature, and wind speed drops off sharply close to the ground. A study of the natural revegetation of disturbed tundra sites on Franconia Ridge, New Hampshire, showed through the use of special traps that seeds rarely carry 3 feet from a parent source. Wind may be more effective in transporting seeds across snow and ice, and some plants like diapensia seem to take advantage of this, shaking their seeds out of persistent capsules that poke stiffly above the thin, windswept snow cover. However, dispersal remains a major obstacle in the spread of alpine plants through sexual reproduction, as neither birds, nor rodents, nor rain waters appear to be any more effective than the wind in getting seeds around.

Once a seed does reach a site suitable for germination, it must survive forbidding problems of establishment. Exposed soil surfaces above the tree-line undergo wide temperature fluctuation daily, especially in the spring and fall, heating up strongly with the absorption of sunlight, but just as rapidly cooling after sundown. When the soil temperature fluctuates back and forth across the freezing point, the soil surface may pulsate up and down by as much as an inch or more, as water in the soil expands upon freezing and then relaxes again with thawing. This intense frost heaving has a disastrous effect on a tiny seedling. It tears roots apart and pushes the seedling out of the ground before it has a chance to establish itself and stabilize the soil. Alpine plants counter this problem to some extent by funneling most of their resources into root growth during the first year, and then switching to greater above-ground development during the second year. Even so, studies show that, on average, only three out of every 100 germinating seedlings will survive to see a second growing season.

It seems, then, that the best way to perpetuate the species under the constraints of the alpine environment is to combine perennial longevity with the prolific seed output more typically seen in annuals. The three percent of the seed population that survives and grows to maturity will maintain some genetic variability in the population, while the year-in and year-out vegetative persistence of perennials assures survival through bad times.

The distance limitations of vegetative reproduction and the problems of seedling establishment in sexual reproduction can make the colonization of bare soils above the treeline a very slow process. These restrictions give rise to concern over a mounting problem in our alpine areas today, as the destruction of alpine vegetation follows from the ever-growing numbers of visitors to our high peaks. As more and more of the high ground is laid bare by trampling and subsequent erosion, and the belowground remnants of former vegetation die off, recovery increasingly depends on successful sexual reproduction. And with the problems that seeds and germinating seedlings face, the establishment of plant cover by this means becomes a game of chance. The odds are best where snow accumulates early and stays late, insulating soil against rapid and frequent freeze-thaw cycles. Elsewhere the development of a critical mass of plant cover, sufficient to stabilize the site and reduce risk to additional recruits, may come only with a succession of unusually good years. Some predictions, based on the data currently available, put recovery time for many of our disturbed alpine areas from several decades to a century or more. It is for this reason, perhaps, that custodians of the High Peaks area in the Adirondacks have introduced hardy, nonnative grasses to stabilize badly eroding sites.

Native alpine species, once established, show a remarkable tolerance for the rigors of their environment through a number of physiological adaptations. It should not be surprising at this point to learn that these plants in general exhibit a prominent shift in their metabolic response to temperature. The optimum temperature for numerous metabolic processes is lower in these plants than for herbs and shrubs of more temperate lowland climes. Whereas maximum photosynthetic rates in low-elevation plants may occur at a temperature of 75 to 85 degrees, in alpine plants photosynthesis may be most efficient at around 55 degrees. Interestingly, though, because alpine plants are often subjected to wide swings in temperature, they are also adapted to adjusting their photosynthetic rates quickly. Just two or three days of warmer weather can cause these plants to shift their optimum temperature for photosynthesis upward so they can maximize their photosynthetic opportunity in the short growing season. As a result, photosynthetic rates at any given time in alpine species may be as high as those in lowland plants. Furthermore, alpine plants can convert starch, the primary product of photosynthesis, into sugar and translocate it to other parts of the plant more efficiently at low temperature than can most other plants.

Low temperature is not the only restriction that alpine vegetation has to adjust to. Even the warm sunny days bring challenges at high elevations, for under these conditions plants in the alpine zone are exposed to relatively high levels of ultraviolet radiation. Just as such exposure may cause severe sunburn on our own skin it can also seriously damage a plant. High doses of ultraviolet radiation cause a number of problems, including the destruction of protein and the breakdown of DNA in the plant. Many plants guard against this danger by producing ultraviolet-absorbing pigments—primarily anthocyanins—in the outer epidermal layers of the leaf. (Recall that anthocyanin is the same pigment that give the leaves of some hardwood trees brilliant color in the fall.) These pigments serve no function in the photosynthetic process, but alpine plants produce them throughout the season to screen ultraviolet radiation before it reaches the inner mesophyll cells of the leaf, where photosynthesis takes place.

The degree to which alpine plants have adapted to their environment is really quite remarkable. In a physiological sense, they are tough and durable—well equipped to deal with the rigors of the high summits. Yet, with the pressure that growing numbers of hikers are putting on these plant communities we are continually reminded of the fragility of alpine vegetation. Is there a paradox here?

It can be argued that no environment is stressful to the organisms that are adapted to it, and such may be the case with alpine vegetation. But tolerance and resilience are two different attributes, and whereas alpine plants exemplify the former, they are quite lacking with regard to the latter. Even though the alpine plant is well adapted to maximizing its growth potential at low temperature, the growing season is, after all, very short and the total plant matter that alpine communities produce in a year is very much less than that for lowland vegetation. We have seen that in this environment getting established initially is extremely difficult. Although a small number of alpine species—most notably the mountain sandwort—display the characteristics of pioneer species, their effectiveness in colonizing alpine sites is very limited compared to the recovery rates that we see following disturbance in the lowlands. Once soil above the treeline is exposed, its loss of biotic potential tends to accelerate rapidly, further delaying the reestablishment of plant cover on it. In the extreme, the combination of loss of organic matter, leaching of nutrients, and an increase in frost heaving leads to the creation of a biological desert. This, too, seems a paradox, but it is something to think about as we hike in the alpine tundra.

## Patterns in Stone

Before leaving this discussion of the alpine environment, we should note some of the interesting topographical features to be found above the treeline. The same climate that shapes the alpine vegetation also creates a number of unique landscape patterns—circular and linear arrangements of stone—that result from the active movement and sorting of rocks under the influence of ice and gravity. Geomorphologists—people who study landforms and the processes that shape them—classify these features as periglacial landforms; the term periglacial refers to a climatic situation that is "almost glacial"—cold enough to support seasonal ground-ice formation and frequent freeze-thaw activity, but not cold enough to sustain permanent snow fields or glaciers. The processes at work in the evolution of these landforms require intense freeze-thaw activity, and for this reason periglacial features are best expressed in our highest alpine areas, where snow cover is thin and where frost stirs ground material not held in place by tree cover.

Periglacial landforms develop under the influence of three basic processes: frost wedging or shattering, seasonal ground ice formation, and mass movement. Frost wedging is the same process that, after deglaciation, left sharp, angular rock rubble on which our subalpine forests perch. Water freezing in bedrock joints or in the minute pores of coarsely grained crystalline rock exerts an enormous force that splits the rock into ever smaller pieces, providing a continuous supply of material that may be moved about by subsequent frost heaving. In the simplest case, this frost shattering leads to the development of extensive block fields (the felsenmeer, or "sea of rocks," that we talked about earlier) that may be in constant, although imperceptible downslope motion (see Figure 22). On steeper slopes the felsenmeer may align into "block streams," where the local topography funnels the rock into channels resembling stream beds (see Figure 23).

The inexorable creep of felsenmeer is encouraged by the freezing of water trapped in the finer materials beneath. As the ice expands, it lifts particles, including the felsenmeer, in a direction perpendicular to the freezing plane (that is, perpendicular to the ground surface), which means that on a slope, the particles are displaced both upward and outward. Upon thawing, they then settle vertically under the influence of gravity, resulting in a net movement downslope of the displaced particles with every freeze-thaw cycle.

Enhancing this process is the development of needle ice in fine-grained soils where an abundant supply of capillary water feeds ice crystals that grow in columns sometimes 3 or 4 inches in height (see Figure 24). In bare soils

**FIGURE 22** Intense frost shattering of bedrock in the alpine zone results in the accumulation of angular fragments on the surface, which are collectively referred to as block fields or felsenmeer.

**FIGURE 23** As frost-shattered rocks move slowly downslope, they are sometimes channeled by the local topography into "block streams."

**FIGURE 24** Needle ice forms in fine-textured soils where there is an abundance of moisture to feed rapidly elongating crystals. The ice grows in a direction perpendicular to the ground plane and is capable of lifting sizable rocks.

**FIGURE 25** Frost ejection of subsurface stones, followed by their slow lateral creep away from centers of high ground, results in the formation of sorted circles or polygons.

**FIGURE 26** In areas of active soil movement, terraces may form wherever downslope creep is temporarily slowed, in effect damming the soil or rock particles. In this situation, the terrace riser is often the only place where plants can establish themselves.

along the trail after the first hard freeze in the fall, needle ice is often seen lifting a cap of soil or rock that will eventually settle downslope from its original position. This downslope creep may also be aided by the flow of saturated soil after thawing, a process known as solifluction.

Freezing activity, whether involving needle ice or not, is also responsible for sorting materials, due to the differential rate of movement of large and small particles. A large rock, lifted up by freezing beneath, often cannot settle back down to its original position after the ground thaws because finer particles, stirred by frost action, have filled in the space underneath. Rocks buried in the subsoil are often brought to the surface by this process of ejection, and once on the surface, even the slightest undulations of topography can result in their being moved laterally by creep.

In the alpine zone, where the stirring of soils by frost is particularly intense and uninhibited by tree roots, this sorting process gives rise to a variety of ground patterns including stone circles, garlands, stripes, steps, and terraces. The circles (actually polygons) occur on uneven but nearly horizontal ground where lateral sorting is active but where there is no sustained downslope movement. Larger particles are moved outward from the centers of hummocks and come to rest in slight hollows or wherever they meet others moving in the opposite direction, thus forming roughly circular netlike patterns under the control of the local topography (see Figure 25). Where a slight slope exists, these circles may migrate slowly downhill, opening up to form crescent-shaped garlands. On steeper slopes the garlands may grade into stripes that run parallel to the direction of the slope.

Wherever the efficiency of downslope creep or solifluction changes such that the soil's movement is slowed, a series of steps or terraces may form. This piling up of soil or rock particles may be caused by changes in vegetation, slope, configuration of the underlying bedrock, or any other factor that results in a change in the intensity of freeze-thaw activity. The steps or terraces thus formed (differences between the two being primarily a matter of scale) may be banked either by coarse rock or by vegetation (see Figure 26).

This simplified discussion belies the complexity of a situation in which many factors act simultaneously on the landscape and where any particular class of ground pattern may have more than one mode of formation. Perhaps the best location in our region for seeing all of these processes at work is in the Alpine Garden and Bigelow Lawn areas of Mount Washington, New Hampshire, where both inactive ("fossil") and presently forming patterns can be found. But anywhere in the alpine regions of the Northeast you might look for patterned ground features, for in this periglacial environment beyond the shelter of the forest, the forces of ice are still paramount in shaping the land.

# CHAPTER 3

# Turning Seasons, Turning Cycles

If there were a single season upon which hinges the success of plant and animal species in the northern forest, it would be autumn. This is a time of crucial preparations for the coming cold, when shortening day-length triggers metabolic and behavioral changes in birds and mammals that will carry them through the winter, when a mere touch of frost stimulates processes that ultimately enable plants to withstand the minus 40-degree and colder temperatures of the northern forest. But autumn is also a time of great importance for the cycling of nutrients and flow of energy that keeps the entire forest ecosystem going. Indeed, the turning and falling of leaves in autumn, with the myriad processes and interactions accompanying it, is an event of monumental proportion.

## WHEN A LEAF FALLS IN THE FOREST

A single dried maple leaf, floating to the ground, weighs only a few hundredths of an ounce. By season's end, however, the collective weight of leaves piling up under an acre of northern hardwoods will approach one-and-a-half tons. Less noticed, our conifers will drop an equivalent amount of litter to the forest floor as they discard older, inefficient foliage in autumn (conifers typically bear more foliage than an equal-sized broadleaf tree). This seasonal windfall of organic matter, when broken down by the countless soil microorganisms awaiting it, will provide energy for many levels of consumers, including small mammals and birds that feed on soil arthropods and earthworms, and will return enough nutrients to the soil to satisfy up to 80 percent of the trees' annual needs. Autumn leaf fall is by no means a haphazard event, though, nor is it the passive process that it may seem. At the plant level, leaf abscission is a complicated matter, not unlike self-amputation. Each leaf represents the endpoint of a long, uninterrupted, vascular connection to the most distant water- and nutrient-gathering root tip, and severing itself from this connection must be accomplished without exposing unprotected vascular tissue to pathogenic fungi and bacteria, or to unimpeded water loss. It is no small task.

The fall of the leaf is, in fact, the very model of planned obsolescence. From the time the leaf emerges in the spring we see signs of preparation for leaf fall, beginning with the development at the cellular level of an abscission zone in the leaf stem, where the leaf will ultimately break from its anchor when its time comes. This abscission zone, consisting of a separation layer—two or more rows of cells at the base of the leaf stem where strengthening tissue is minimal—and a protective, wound-healing tissue several cells thick adjacent to the separation layer, is strong enough to support the leaf throughout the growing season, but it begins to weaken with chemical changes occurring in cells during early autumn.

Prior to leaf fall, deciduous and evergreen trees and shrubs begin to shift their metabolic activities from one set of processes associated with active growth and reproduction to another associated with cold-season acclimation. As leaves start to turn, metabolites and mineral elements, many of which are recovered from the breakdown of cellular components, begin to move out of the leaves and into more permanent tissues in the stems and roots of the tree. Plant hormones are redistributed, membranes are altered, and carbohydrate reserves are shuttled into storage. Even while growth processes are shutting down, the mitochondrial engines of the leaf's cells keep plugging away, providing the energy for this active redistribution of materials, until finally the leaf is ready to drop. Water movement slows, the conducting cells in the abscission layer start to clog, and cellular bonds begin to dissolve. A breeze stirs and the leaf breaks away.

Before the leaf falls, however, there is another story to tell. It is a fascinating story of species interactions—of a remarkable association between the leaf and the very fungi that may initiate its decomposition. It is a story of microbial succession, not unlike our earlier description of forest community succession, but on a miniature scale. And, like the brief account of leaf abscission above, it is a story that begins long before leaf fall.

The moment a new leaf pokes out from its bud, it becomes a target for all manner of organisms. This is a simple fact of plant life, for green leaves are

## Fall Colors

THE GREEN LEAVES of summer harbor more than meets the eye, for beneath their veil of chlorophyll hides an impressive array of colorful pigments—carotenoids and phycobilins that are yellow, orange, and red. We don't see much of these pigments in summer because they are swamped by the sheer abundance of chlorophyll, but they are present throughout the season and serve an important function in the leaf. These "accessory" pigments trap light in portions of the spectrum not absorbed by chlorophyll and transfer this energy to the chlorophyll molecules, thereby increasing the efficiency of the photosynthetic process.

During the growing season, chlorophyll is constantly being produced and simultaneously broken down into simpler compounds. In the fall of the year, however, when temperatures drop, chlorophyll molecules in deciduous leaves are no longer replaced and the green begins to fade. Only then are the brilliant colors of the other pigments unmasked. As growth processes throughout the tree slow and the translocation of metabolites out of the leaves diminishes, sugars that are no longer in demand accumulate in the leaves, where they stimulate production in some species of yet another non-photosynthetic pigment called anthocyanin. Anthocyanin is bright red in color and is produced in the vacuole or central void of the epidermal cells that make up the leaf's outer layers. Oddly, anthocyanin seems of little benefit to the leaf at this time of year (it has no known function in the senescing leaf), but it certainly does much for us as it fires up the fall colors that dress our hardwood forests in magnificence.

the source of chemical energy for all other consumers. But leaves—especially broad ones—also provide a convenient platform upon which many other organisms, particularly fungi, might better carry out their own life processes. And these hitchhikers waste little time finding the new leaf.

Fungi disperse via tiny, wind-borne spores and the constant deposition of these spores from the atmosphere means they can show up just about anywhere. Indeed, yeast cells—unicellular fungi—may even be found within the very bud scales that protect the developing leaf over winter. This means that new leaves often emerge in the spring already seeded with colonial fungi. The yeasts in this case are innocuous, deriving their energy from organic dust particles or from sugars leaking from epidermal cells of the young leaf, and

**FIGURE 27** Common litter decomposers of spruce-fir forests (left column) and northern hardwood forests (right column). From top to bottom, left: *Hygrophoropsis aurantiaca, Paxillus atrotomentosus, Ganoderma tsugae*. From top to bottom, right: *Trametes versicolor, Xeromphalina kauffmanii, Crepidotus applanatus*.

pose no burden to the plant. But they are the pioneers and a harbinger of things to come. In little time, other windborne fungal spores will join them on the leaf surface, and this is where the interesting interactions begin.

With billions of spores floating in the air, the arrival of different fungal species on a leaf surface is entirely random. Like wind-dispersed seeds of plants alighting on a patch of bare ground, some of the early arriving fungi will find the new leaf surface a suitable environment for their establishment—a fruitful platform from which to scavenge organic debris with minimal competition for resources—while others will find the leaf inhospitable and soon perish in the drought-prone and nutrient-deficient environment. And those that become established first may exert strong influence over subsequent arrivals, just as we saw with forest succession (page 13). Many fungi, for example, exude antagonistic substances that inhibit the establishment of additional colonies nearby. In addition, fungi frequently protect themselves from insect grazers by producing strong alkaloids that interfere with insect larval development, sometimes even killing larvae outright. (Though the fungus is merely looking out for itself, these interactions directly benefit the plant as well, since the presence of the fungal colonists may substantially reduce the burden of leaf-chewing caterpillars.)

The early colonizers may be able to defend their space on the leaf for a while, but by late summer the deposition of fungal spores becomes increasingly heavy. The leaf may now host several thousand spores per square inch. Other species begin to thrive as the aging epidermal cells leak more metabolites and increasing amounts of pollen dust the surface (pollen is another ready source of energy for the saprophytic fungi). Species interactions become more intense, the balance of competition shifts, and the early colonists slowly give way to a new community of fungi—a community more saprophytic in its nature, thriving on dead organic matter. The inevitable fate of the leaf is foretold high in the forest canopy.

Riding the leaf to the ground, then, is a colony of fungi already established on the leaf surface. Some of these fungi will prosper in the more humid and stable environment of the forest floor and play a role in initial decomposition of the leaves, while others will fade quietly away, completing their life cycle largely unnoticed. On the ground, the composition of the fungal community shifts once more. The task of recycling the bulk of this organic

## The Life Net Beneath Us

FUNGI MAY WELL be the most underappreciated players among the cast of characters that make up our northern forest. Occasionally identified as a disease organism (see "Beech Bark Disease" on page 73), the vast majority of fungal species are non-parasitic saprophytes that earn their living breaking down dead organic matter.

The body of a fungus consists of a branching network of thread-like cells called hyphae. As these cells divide and explore the organic landscape, they secrete extracellular enzymes that dissolve cellulose and lignin, notoriously resistant components of plant matter, and absorb the products of decomposition into their hyphae. Nutrients and energy thus garnered are passed along the food web as numerous other grazers in the soil feed upon the fungal hyphae.

Not all fungi are free-living. Some unite with algae to form lichens (see page 120), and some have evolved mycorrhizal (often called "fungus root") relationships with living plant hosts. In the latter case, the fungal partner, taking up residence in the plant root, taps the host for carbohydrates, but benefits the host by garnering nutrients more efficiently, via its extensive hyphal network, than do plant roots alone.

The presence of fungi in the forest litter goes largely unnoticed until the fungi reproduce. The spore-producing mushroom develops only when one probing hyphal strand encounters another of compatible type and fuses or grafts with it. Once the hyphae are paired, further development of the fruiting body awaits the proper environmental cue—usually an abundance of moisture. This is why mushrooms commonly show up in autumn, when the number of days with recorded precipitation in the Northeast increases noticeably.

Thin and inconspicuous though they may be, the hyphal network of some litter-decomposing fungi can reach gigantic proportions. Researchers have traced the hyphae of a single clone of *Armillaria bulbosa* (all *Armillaria* species are known as "honey mushrooms") under 36 acres of hardwood forest in Michigan and estimated its total weight conservatively at 100 tons! Billed immediately as one of the world's largest living organisms, its title was quickly upended by another *Armillaria* behemoth found in southwestern Washington that covered 1,500 acres. This, in turn, was followed by the discovery in eastern Oregon of an *Armillaria* individual underlying 2,384 acres—the current record holder for world's largest known organism.

If all this were not impressive enough, a microbiologist from Tufts University Medical School, Moselio Schaechter, has estimated that fungal biomass worldwide averages just under a half ton per acre for all the vegetated land on earth, adding up to nearly 2 tons for every person on the planet!

windfall now belongs primarily to the class of litter-dwelling fungi known as Basidiomycetes that form many familiar gilled mushrooms. These are the real heavy hitters, equipped with the enzymes necessary to break down the tough lignins, cellulose, and strong defense compounds of the plant leaf. While they do not act alone—it takes the collective cutting, grinding, and digesting of myriad soil organisms to break the litter into smaller particles, exposing more surface area to the enzymatic action of the fungi—it is the Basidiomycetes that ultimately close the loop in the recycling process (see "The Life Net Beneath Us" on page 136 and Figure 27).

Behind the turning of leaves, countless other changes are also occurring during autumn. Almost every plant and animal in the northern forest is preparing for winter in one way or another, some conspicuously, others invisible to us. By the time all the leaves have fallen, trees and shrubs will have acquired the ability to withstand deep freezing—a complex physiological transformation triggered in late summer by shortening day length and bolstered with the first frosts of autumn. Insects, too, will have completed preparations for the coming cold, some avoiding freezing altogether, even to extreme low temperatures, through a combination of behavioral and chemical means, and others making necessary physiological adjustments to accommodate a remarkable amount of ice formation in their bodies. The story is much the same for the Northeast's amphibians and reptiles, with some—dusky salamanders, red-spotted newts, and American toads, for example—seeking safe places where they are unlikely to experience sub-freezing temperatures (they have no freezing tolerance). Others, like the spring peeper, gray treefrog, wood frog, and painted turtle hatchling, acquire the ability to withstand limited ice formation in their body tissues without harm.

Many birds will have already departed for southern climates, not so much for lack of cold tolerance on their part, but rather because of an impending scarcity of food as insects become inactive or metamorphose into resting forms. The first few frosts will also have readied hibernators for their long metabolic journey—as perilous a journey as migration, for the risks of hibernation are many and mortality, especially among juveniles, can be high. For others that will face winter head-on, physiological adjustments for the coming cold—the addition of insulating layers, changes in basal metabolic rate, increased capacity to generate heat from shivering or from brown fat

**WOOD FROG *(Rana sylvatica)***
Most widely distributed amphibian in North America, ranging from the Appalachian Mountains to arctic treeline in Canada and Alaska. Adult is terrestrial, seeking temporary pools for breeding in early spring (often before ice has completely melted). Active by day; males call females during mating with a duck-like quack. Hibernates under shallow organic litter, where it survives freezing.

**AMERICAN TOAD**
***(Bufo americanus)*** A habitat generalist, requiring moist environments and temporary water for breeding. Male's mating call is a melodious high-pitched trill lasting about 30 seconds. Primarily nocturnal with a voracious appetite for insects. Escapes freezing by digging backwards into soil with hind feet.

**SPRING PEEPER *(Pseudacris crucifer)*** Able to climb, though mostly found on the ground. Gathers in large numbers for breeding at ephemeral pools just after ice melts. Frogs may freeze and thaw nightly at beginning of the breeding season. Mating call of the male is a loud peep, with the chorus of many frogs audible at dusk for more than a mile.

**NORTHERN DUSKY SALAMANDER**
*(Desmognathus fuscus)* Prefers running or trickling water; rarely strays from woodland streams, seeps, or springs. Often found under flat rocks, logs, or wet leaves. Female deposits eggs in small pools and remains with the eggs until they hatch in late summer. Young are born with gills.

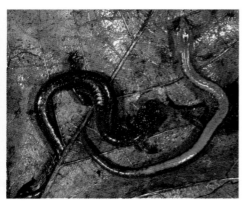

**RED-BACKED SALAMANDER**
*(Plethodon cinereus)* Found in two color forms, with and without the red stripe on back. Must maintain moist skin at all times, but does not spend any part of its life cycle in water. Eggs are laid in a cluster beneath a rock or log, guarded by female for two months. Young are born looking like miniature adults. Active mostly at night.

**RED-SPOTTED NEWT**
*(Notophthalmus viridescens)* Pond-dwelling adults are olive on top with red and black spots, yellow underneath. Young leave water in late summer for a terrestrial phase where it becomes known as a "red eft" (pictured here), inhabiting moist woodlands. Returns to water after two or three years to complete life as an adult.

metabolism—are progressing safely in advance of the season, triggered, as with plants, by shortening day length.

Birds and mammals that remain active during the winter season are confronted with an unpredictable food supply at a time when energy needs are highest. Many will make it through the winter only because of their ability to store sufficient energy reserves at this time of year—either in the form of body fat or stockpiled food. Birds show an extraordinary ability to add small amounts of fat quickly, an adaptation, in part, to the weight-limitations imposed by flight, but only a few in the Northeast—notably jays, chickadees, nuthatches, and shrikes—actively cache food. (Some owls may cache food during temporary times of prey abundance. Great horned, boreal, and saw-whet owls have been known to cache prey in winter and thaw the prey by "incubating" them as they would eggs!) Mammals add body fat almost universally, either as a layer of subcutaneous white fat that provides some insulation in addition to serving as an energy reserve, or as local deposits of brown adipose tissue concentrated near the vital organs and having an extraordinary capacity to generate heat when metabolized. However, since smaller mammals are also limited by their size in the amount of fat they can add, they often must supplement their fat stores by hoarding food.

Several mammals in the northern forest stash food to one degree or another. Voles will stockpile just about anything manageable—roots, stems, and leaves of herbaceous plants, fruits, nuts, and fungi—usually waiting until snow hides their activity and then gathering foodstuffs into larders where it is more accessible to their communal nests beneath the winter snowpack. Flying squirrels also share communal nests in winter and stuff tree cavities with buds, catkins, nuts, seeds, fruits, mushrooms, lichens, and insect larvae. The often arboreal deer mice, with a similarly varied diet, likewise hoard seeds, nuts, and fruits in tree hollows (just how often the two species discover each other's food caches is not known). In contrast to these "larder" hoarders, the solitary shrews, weasels, mink, and foxes tend to stash excess prey items singly throughout their territories—a habit termed "scatter-hoarding." Scatter hoarding is more common among animals that do not remain in one place to defend their caches, the advantage ostensibly being to reduce potential losses should a cache be discovered and robbed. The likelihood of discovery by another animal, though, seems minimal. Studies of foxes have suggested that prey recovery is based almost entirely upon memory, rather than sense of smell. In experimental enclosures where two or more foxes had been allowed to cache mice, individuals proved adept at recovering their own stashes, but rarely found prey cached by another.

Easily the most visible food hoarding activities of the season are those of beaver and red squirrels, the former with its large stockpile of brush outside the entrance to its lodge, and the latter with its conspicuous middens of buried spruce and fir cones. Both mammals are dietary specialists, with the beaver feeding on the inner bark of woody trees and shrubs and the red squirrel acquiring most of its energy during winter from the seeds of spruce and fir trees. (At other times of the year, the red squirrel is an opportunistic feeder.) And though these two animals differ significantly in habit and habitat, each faces a similar challenge during winter: limited access to a single food item. Once ice forms on the pond, the beaver will no longer have access to the woody vegetation on shore, and once the spruce and fir cones high in the tree tops release their seeds to the wind, the red squirrel will no longer have access to a concentrated food source.

The beaver solves its problem by harvesting branches of willows, alders, almost any shrub or tree growing nearby, and "planting" the stems—often several hundred (researchers have actually counted them to determine energy content)—in the mud of the pond bottom, or sometimes just gathering them into a floating "raft," the bulk of it underwater, that eventually becomes anchored in the ice. These food caches are usually quite conspicuous in the fall, protruding from the water, leaves often still on, close to the underwater entrance to the lodge (see Figure 28).

The red squirrel solves its problem by harvesting cones before they open, burying them by the thousands in the organic soil of the forest floor where moisture will keep the cone scales tightly closed, preventing loss of the seeds. And the squirrel does this with unmatched energy, darting to the tops of the tallest trees, clipping cones and dropping them to the ground, scurrying down to round them up and then burying them in moist duff. The squirrel's larder may be concentrated in one or a few middens—deep piles of organic debris resulting from repeated dismantling of cones in favored feeding locations—or scattered throughout its territory in smaller clusters. Almost unfailingly,

**FIGURE 28** Beaver prepare for a long winter under ice by caching food—freshly cut tree and shrub branches—near the entrance of their lodge. Here, leaves still show on the cuttings being stockpiled to the right of the lodge.

the red squirrel will locate these stores weeks or months later via a network of tunnels beneath the winter snowpack.

Red squirrels also have a penchant for hoarding mushrooms in autumn. As if to waste neither opportunity nor motion, the squirrel, in its cone-gathering frenzy, can often be seen scampering back up the tree with a mushroom in its mouth. The mushroom would not last long buried in the soil, and the squirrel seems to understand this, so it wedges the morsel into the crotch of a branch high in the tree (or deposits it in a vacant bird nest!) where the mushroom will air-dry and last until it is retrieved—or discovered by some other hungry fungivore.

While the constraints of winter hunting or foraging are obvious and the advantages of caching food clear, it is important to note that hoarding alone is rarely sufficient to secure the future of the animal. Indeed, as we will see in a moment, animals employ a number of strategies in winter to reduce their food needs as well. There are two sides to every energy budget and almost invariably, food hoarding behavior is tightly coupled with critical energy-conserving adaptations.

# SIX MONTHS OF WINTER

With the leaves down and food stores established, preparations for winter are nearly complete. The behavior of all animals, hunters and hunted alike, is dictated now by the cold and the need to obtain or conserve energy. Until the snow cover arrives, life will be more difficult for some, easier for others. But once the snowpack is in place, life will change for all.

For those animals that remain active throughout winter, snow is either a blessing or a curse. Deepening snow buffers the vole from the vagaries of winter weather, shelters the grouse on a cold night, and elevates the snow-shoe hare to new sources of food. Deepening snow forces the bear into its den, pushes the wild turkey into open farmland in search of waste grain, and cripples the white-tail deer, restricting its movement severely and relegating it largely to a winter of fasting. In the balance, however, the remarkable level of activity that we observe during the winter tells us that plants and animals of the northern forest are superbly well-adjusted to the season (even the deer's fasting is adaptive), and it is hard to imagine the northern forest without its long, deep winter.

To some extent, the beaver and the red squirrel exemplify the range of challenges and the strategies employed, both physiological and behavioral, by smaller mammals to survive winter. While the beaver is unique in its aquatic confinement during winter (the semi-aquatic muskrat is not entirely restricted to life under ice), its challenges—and advantages—are not unlike those of other communal nesters whose food resources are limited and are shared with nest mates. Beavers remain minimally active during winter, taking advantage of the relative warmth of their lodge and huddling lodge-mates (a pair of adults and up to four kits may be present in the lodge over winter) to reduce their energy requirements significantly. Even so, the amount of food stockpiled by beavers is rarely enough to satisfy the total energetic needs of the lodge occupants for the winter. It appears instead that the food cache is primarily for the benefit of the kits, with the adults of the lodge fasting for much of the winter, subsisting mostly on fat reserves stored in the tail (kits have been reported to gain weight during winter, while adults often lose weight, their tail shrinking as fat is utilized). It is a strategy that seems to work well, however. Beaver often remain locked under the ice for weeks after winter has relaxed its hold on the land, yet they rarely succumb to the season.

For the solitary red squirrel, winter's challenges are quite different. One of the more familiar animals of our winter woods, the squirrel is surprisingly ill-equipped for the cold. Its small body size renders it twice disadvantaged: It loses heat quickly to its cold surroundings and at the same time is limited in its ability to increase insulation. Though the squirrel may actually double its fur thickness going into winter, its rate of heat loss is still such that it must constantly fuel its metabolic furnace in order to maintain normal body temperature, even on the warmest winter days. This disadvantage is partially offset by the squirrel's ability—shared by most small mammals—to accumulate deposits of brown fat around the vital organs, where the remarkable heat-producing capability of this specialized tissue is most effective. Distinctly different from white fat (it looks more like a gland than a layer of fat), brown adipose tissue possesses abundant mitochondria (the metabolic engines of the cell) and a rich blood supply, and is capable of exceptional rates of oxidation and heat production—so much so that temperatures measured over local brown fat deposits have been known to exceed core body temperature.

But this remarkable heat generator requires an abundance of fuel, since the red squirrel remains active through all but the coldest days of winter. Not surprisingly, then, most of the squirrel's winter activity is centered on recovering cones from its extensive stores. How large are these stores, and how much does it take for the squirrel to survive winter? It has been estimated that the energy needs of a red squirrel during a typical temperate-zone winter may approach 15,000 kilocalories. At an average of 2,500 calories per cone, depending on tree species, a squirrel may need in excess of 6,000 cones to get through winter!

Several other small, solitary animals face the same dilemma as the red squirrel—namely, a high cooling rate and the need to obtain large quantities of food. Shrews are a particularly good example, with one member of this family, the pygmy shrew, approaching the smallest body size theoretically feasible for a warm-blooded animal (any smaller and it wouldn't be able to eat enough to match heat loss from its tiny body). Shrews must hunt almost constantly beneath the snowpack during winter, taking anything from spiders and insects to other small mammals (shrew species vary almost ten-fold in size, with the larger ones able to take occasional mice and voles). Weasels, too, seem to be built inappropriately for winter. Long and thin, with short fur and little fat, they are poorly adapted to conserving heat and yet are among the most active of winter residents in the northern forest. In their thin bodies, however, we see a tradeoff between heat loss and hunting efficiency. Weasels are built for pursuing quarry in tight spaces, and they do this with unmatched efficiency, consuming in excess of one-quarter of their body weight in food each day. Weasels also offset some of their energetic disadvantage by spending a considerable amount of time beneath the snow, through which they travel easily, gaining some protection from the cold air above. The weasel's white winter coat provides additional insulation as well, since the white hairs are partially hollow, lacking the dark, granular pigments of the summer coat.

If shrews, weasels, and red squirrels represent one end of the winter adaptation spectrum, the northern forest's white-tailed deer and moose would be situated at the other—and not just because of their size difference. Deer and moose are ruminants, and that carries an important advantage during long winters. The ability to digest woody material in the rumen, a specialized fermentation chamber (often referred to as a second stomach), gives these animals access to almost unlimited food during winter. This is coupled with a second advantage. The digestive activity of bacteria in the rumen generates a significant amount of heat beyond that which the animal produces during normal resting metabolism. For deer or moose, this amounts to free heat.

But there's a down side to this, as well. While woody material may be abundant in winter, its nutritional value can be quite poor when compared to the quality of summer forage with its high content of protein and soluble carbohydrate. Toughened by an excess of structural material, the winter stems are mostly hard-to-digest lignin and cellulose, which requires more time to break down in the rumen. So, in spite of the ready availability of winter food, the amount of material a deer or moose can process in winter is limited by the length of time it takes to digest it, which is why deer have been known to die from malnutrition with their stomachs full.

The large size of deer and moose offsets, to some extent, the limitations imposed by a diet consisting entirely of woody stems. The advantage, in this case, is related to the animal's ability to store energy in the form of fat. As an animal increases in size, its capacity to accumulate fat becomes proportionately greater than the rate at which it metabolizes the reserve energy. Whereas a small animal usually has a narrow margin between its fat storage capacity and its rate of consumption—and therefore has to eat more frequently—a larger animal with sufficient reserves can fast and still remain warm for longer periods, breaking down the stored fat without having to forage for food. This ability turns out to be of critical importance to deer during a long winter, for getting to food in deep snow can become problematic and may consume more energy than the deer recovers from feeding.

When a deer begins to move about in the snow, the amount of energy it expends increases exponentially with snow depth and density (as the latter affects food drag). The very act of standing, in fact, exposes a deer to higher energy costs in winter. The long, thin legs of the deer present a large surface area which, when exposed to the cold, can result in a 20 percent or greater increase in metabolic rate simply to offset the additional heat loss. Thus, for the deer, balancing the daily energy budget comes down to a choice of either increasing foraging effort to compensate for the lower quality of food and higher energy requirements of moving about, or minimizing foraging to conserve energy, relying instead on fat reserves accumulated earlier in the year to make it through winter. And it is the latter that usually wins out. By midwinter, we often see deer congregating in areas of dense conifers, where snow is shallower and their collective trampling makes movement somewhat easier. But food is soon depleted in the vicinity of such "deer yards," and conserving energy by fasting quickly becomes the key to survival.

Moose are less inclined to seek the shallower snow beneath conifers. They have a height advantage and a musculature that enables them to raise their legs high and move through deep snow with considerably less energy expenditure than deer. Nonetheless, moose tend to limit their activities in order to conserve energy, seeking winter habitat, often streamside, that offers a high concentration of shrubs within a relatively small area. Lacking sufficient riparian habitat, they will seek out clearings within conifer forests that have abundant birch and aspen saplings. In times of especially deep snow, moose will browse on lower quality balsam fir and subsidize their energy needs from fat reserves, rather than move to new areas for deciduous browse. Factoring into this behavior, however, is another significant adaptation: The insulation of a moose's winter coat is superior to that of any other mammal in the northern forest, imparted in large measure by extremely long guard hairs (at 4 inches in length, they nearly double those of the white-tailed deer). This translates into an ability to maintain normal body temperature, without having to elevate its metabolic rate, in air temperatures as low as minus 25 degrees—a 20-degree advantage over the white-tailed deer. Indeed, moose are so well adapted to the cold that some biologists believe warm temperatures and heat stress during the summer set the southern limits of their distribution.

Thus we see there are a number of different solutions to the challenges animals face during our northern winters—not a single "best" answer, but each suited to the life history of the animal in question. Indeed, overwinter success depends on the entire suite of adaptations by which an animal is best able to exploit the resources of its environment, while at the same time avoiding predation. There is no better way to appreciate the challenges and adaptive behaviors of animals in winter than to follow their tracks in the snow, paying careful attention to details: What is the distance between track impressions? Is the animal traveling quickly or is it moving slowly and deliberately? Is it probing openings in the snow cover, exploring from tree to tree or shrub to shrub? Or is it moving more directly as if to get from one place to another, as if traveling between similar habitat types or between bedding and feeding areas? Is it browsing on plants, digging in the snow, seeking shelter? Careful observation of tracks in the snow will tell much about how well—or poorly—the animal is doing.

For inhabitants of the forest floor, life in the Northeast would be considerably more difficult without dependable snow cover. Without snow, frost penetrates deeply into the soil, perennial plants suffer from the drying effects of exposure, small mammals burn critical energy reserves and are more vulnerable to predators, and hibernating reptiles and amphibians are threatened with freezing. But how much snow does it take to make a difference? The answer depends on one critical aspect of the snow—its density.

Snow on the ground is a mixture of ice crystals and air, and the relative amount of the two determines its density. The amount of air entrapped in the snowpack is greatest (therefore density is lowest) right after a snowfall. Within a few hours, however, the snow becomes compacted as ice crystals lose their delicate structure and settle closer to each other. Air volume is reduced, and snowpack density increases. This settling is facilitated by physical forces such

**WEASEL** Hind feet land in impressions left by front feet, creating paired tracks, with one side (right or left) leading the other slightly. Leaps alternately clear the surface and drag in the snow, creating a characteristic "dumbbell" pattern. Tracks reflect energetic activity as weasel darts from place to place, commonly disappearing into, or emerging from, holes in the snow.

**AMERICAN MARTEN** Similar to weasel (a large member of the same family), showing characteristic paired prints with right or left foot leading the other, but substantially larger than weasel and not showing "dumbbell" pattern. Tracks often seen on leaning, snow-covered tree trunks, as the marten hunts both on the ground and in trees.

**SNOWSHOE HARE** When bounding, the fore feet fall in line, one behind the other, with the outsized hind feet landing well forward and even with each other. In this photo, the hare was moving toward the viewer. Distance between track impressions can be several feet when the hare senses danger.

**RED SQUIRREL** On firm snow, pattern is typical of hopping animals, with larger hind feet landing outside and forward of front feet. Soft snow may obscure this pattern, showing only two larger impressions side-by-side. Streaks between sets of prints are common in fresh snow. Tracks from tree to tree and in and out of tunnels in the snow help identify track as red squirrel.

**COYOTE** Difficult to distinguish from domestic dogs, except by behavior. Tracks tend to be neater, with hind feet placed in impressions left by fore feet in an effort to conserve energy. Following tracks for some distance will give clues to hunting activity. Fox tracks are similar, but dainty by comparison.

**PORCUPINE** In soft snow, plows a deep trough, remaining visible even after subsequent snowfalls. Trough often leads from one tree to the next, as porcupine samples and eventually climbs a tree for extended feeding. On firm snow, the pigeon-toed track and drag marks of the heavily quilled tail are distinctive.

as wind pressure and the weight of additional snow, but air temperature is of overriding importance. Snow crystals retain their structure much longer at low temperatures, so colder air generally means lighter snow. Conversely, as temperatures warm, the transformation of snow crystals to rounded ice grains accelerates, the grains pack closer together, and density increases. As snowpack density increases, the snow becomes less effective as an insulating blanket.

Generally speaking, 8 inches of fresh snow is enough to dampen temperature fluctuations at ground level. But "fresh" is an ephemeral condition, especially in a winter climate that vacillates between extreme cold and above-freezing temperatures. As the snowpack settles, it takes a greater depth to compensate for the increase in density, and in the Northeast the environment of the forest floor doesn't become isolated from weather conditions above the snow until it reaches an average depth of approximately 16 to 20 inches (given typical densities of snow in the northern forest).

Once the snowpack is established and temperatures stabilize beneath the snow, additional changes begin to take place that will shape life in this underworld. With the bottom of the snowpack now warmer than its upper reaches (ground-level temperature will remain close to the freezing point throughout winter), ice grains at the base of the snowpack begin to undergo yet another transformation, this time losing strength and forming brittle, cup-like crystals with the bonds between them barely holding together. Space begins to open up at the base of the snowpack as these fragile crystals eventually dissipate altogether; the snowpack becomes suspended, supported by downed trees, shrubs, and saplings of the forest floor; and animals are free to move relatively unimpeded.

But increasing depth and density of the snowpack also brings perpetual darkness to the forest floor. Ninety percent or more of the light striking the surface of a clean snowpack is reflected, and most of that which passes through the surface is absorbed quickly within the upper layers. Only about one-tenth of 1 percent of the light penetrating the surface makes it to the forest floor. It is an important fraction though, for it is radiant energy of just the right wavelength for plant receptors, and that has important implications for later.

Throughout most of the winter, then, plants and animals beneath the snowpack operate in darkness. Nonetheless, life goes on. Insects and spiders explore the leaf litter. Voles forage from their communal nests. Shrews and weasels hunt. The animals of the forest floor are utilizing the full complement of their physiological and behavioral strategies now. The insulation provided by the snowpack compensates in large measure for the animals' lack of it. Nest materials add still more protection. Voles that have abandoned the aggressions of their earlier, solitary existence are reaping the benefits of communal nesting. Huddling with nest mates reduces heat loss and allows an animal to return to a warm nest after a round of foraging. The autumn weight loss of the voles in preparation for winter reduces their food needs, minimizing competition with nest mates. Brown fat metabolism does the rest. Under the cover of snow, our studies tell us, the animals seem to do well.

Remarkably, by early March signs of impending spring begin to appear beneath the snowpack. Even under the deepest of snow, plants start to show new life. A few seeds germinate. Early perennials like the spring beauty and dogtooth violet sprout from underground tubers. Chlorophyll appears in leaves. Flower buds develop. And long before the snow disappears, the voles, too, start behaving as though it were spring, awakening sexually and beginning to reproduce. But with unwavering temperature under as much as 6 feet of snow, how do the plants and animals know that spring is on the way?

We noted earlier that only a tiny fraction of the light falling on the surface of the snow is able to penetrate to any depth during midwinter. This begins to change, however, as soon as snow starts to melt on the surface. When meltwater percolates downward from the surface and reaches the colder layers below (warming of the snowpack interior is delayed by the insulating snow above it), it refreezes, forming an ice layer in which small ice grains are fused together into larger masses with fewer air spaces. This slightly alters the light-transmitting properties of the snowpack, since light can now pass through this ice layer with less deflection and absorption. And plants beneath the snowpack, with their impressive collection of photoreceptors—pigment molecules that are sensitive to changing light quality and quantity and that control the timing of many plant processes—may be the first to detect the subtle change. It is quite possible, then, that plants serve as an intermediary in stimulating the voles' spring-like behavior. Chemicals that regulate growth in plants—hormones, for example, present in germinating seeds and growing young plants—have been shown to directly stimulate reproductive activity in small mammals that ingest them, suggesting that the voles may be getting their cues from the plants they eat. Thus plants, as receptors of light energy and mediators of biochemical change in animals, may be the ultimate harbinger of spring beneath our winter snowpack.

# CHAPTER 4

# An Atmosphere of Change

Our discussion of the northern forest began with a consideration of landscape changes following retreat of the continental ice sheet from the area some 10,000 years ago. As the ice gradually waned, the newly exposed, barren ground was slowly invaded by treeless tundra vegetation resembling much of today's arctic. Close on its heels, the spruce-fir forests migrated northward from their glacial refugia, establishing themselves first in the valleys and then gradually moving up the hillsides, pushing the tundra vegetation upward. As the climate steadily warmed, the northern hardwoods eventually arrived in the Northeast, displacing in turn much of the spruce-fir on mid-elevation slopes. With some fluctuation in relative dominance over time, and with some movement up and down in elevation, these three distinctive vegetation types established a new balance with the region's climate to become the northern forest as we now know it.

After a relatively stable equilibrium for the past 2,000 years, however, the picture seems to be changing again. Over the last two decades, numerous published reports have cited evidence of advancing treelines throughout the northern hemisphere, including documentation of abundant seedling establishment above existing treelines and sustained increases in radial growth of mature trees at the forest edge. And now we have evidence that several tree species common to the northern forest are starting to push northward from the center of their distributions. Many land birds have shifted their ranges northward as well, as have some important insect and disease vectors. With change in the air, it seems appropriate to close our discussion with another look at the landscape in relation to a warming climate.

## CLIMATE IN QUESTION

In 1958, C. David Keeling of the Scripps Institute of Oceanography established a facility at the Mauna Loa Observatory in Hawaii for precisely monitoring carbon dioxide levels in the atmosphere. At that time, scientists were just beginning to take an interest in the potential effects of fluctuating $CO_2$ concentrations on Earth's climate, related to the disproportionately large capacity of $CO_2$ to trap heat in our atmosphere. The facility Keeling started has provided an uninterrupted record of $CO_2$ levels for 60 years—and in that short time period, we have seen $CO_2$ in our atmosphere increase by 25 percent to the highest levels ever recorded.

To put the Mauna Loa data in perspective, scientists have since begun analyzing air samples trapped for centuries in the glacial ice of Antarctica and Greenland, developing a record of atmospheric $CO_2$ fluctuations going back several hundred millennia in time. (The different strata from which air samples are extracted can be dated with considerable accuracy, much like the way trees can be dated by their annual rings.) The picture that has emerged shows that the current trend in rising $CO_2$ began in the late 1870s, when atmospheric concentrations were at about three-fourths of the present level. The data also show that carbon-dioxide concentrations have increased at a faster rate during the last century than for any period over the past 1,000 years. All indications are that current levels of atmospheric $CO_2$ are higher than at any time in the past 700,000 years.

Climate changes consistent with the increase in concentrations of this heat-trapping gas have already been observed in the Northeast. While mean annual temperature across the Northeast has risen more than 1.5 degrees since 1970, winters have warmed more than 4 degrees in the same period, accompanied by greater winter rainfall, a thinner snowpack, and increased snow density. Ice on lakes and rivers is forming later in autumn and breaking up sooner in spring, the length of the growing season has increased, leaf and bloom dates are earlier for some species, and significant range extensions of plants and animals are occurring. Interestingly, several sophisticated climate models predicted the warming trend recorded over the past century, as well as the accelerated warming that has been observed since 1970, though with a slight tendency to underestimate the degree of change actually witnessed. It is noteworthy that these same models consistently underestimated the rapid *winter* warming that has occurred across the Northeast since 1970.

With long-range climate forecasts projecting continued warming, it would appear that the stage is set for a new wave of vegetation changes with profound implications for the northern forest. Under the most conservative climate change scenarios, which assume reduced carbon dioxide emissions in the future, temperatures in our area are expected to continue rising, warming by nearly 2.4 degrees on average over the next 30 years and 5 degrees by the end of the century. Temperature increases during the winter months are expected to be greater than the annual average, with warming during the summers lower than the annual average. Along with these expected temperature changes, the Northeast is likely to experience an increase in humidity, such that, from a human perspective, our northern forest region will begin to "feel" much more like the southern Appalachians (see Figure 29).

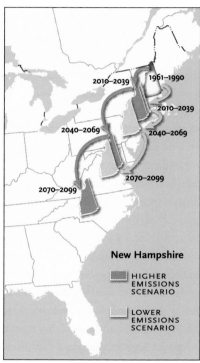

**FIGURE 29** Projected increases in summer heat and humidity for the Adirondack region and northern New England are depicted here by comparing the future climate of upstate New York and New Hampshire to the present climate of Atlantic coast states. The higher emissions scenario assumes atmospheric CO2 will triple that of pre-industrial levels by 2100; the lower scenario assumes a doubling of pre-industrial levels. (Adapted, with permission, from "Climate Change in the U. S. Northeast: A Report of the Northeast Climate Impact Assessment," Union of Concerned Scientists, October 2007.)

## SPECIES ON THE MOVE

If our climate begins to "feel" more like that of the southern Appalachians, will our northern forest region also begin to look more like the southern Appalachians? The answer would seem an inevitable "Yes." The makeup of a forest community at any point in time generally reflects the outcome of competitive interactions between species (the coexisting species able to successfully divide the resources of the site among themselves). A significant change in climate is likely to bring about a shift in this competitive balance as factors like soil temperature, moisture, and nutrient status are altered, resulting in a different set of "winners" (recall our earlier discussion of forest succession on page 13). Such change appears to be under way already. In a research effort of enormous proportion, six government and university collaborators and hundreds of field personnel analyzed data in 2009 on the latitudinal distribution of seedlings and mature trees for a number of northern species, discovering that almost every species common to the northern forest is establishing seedlings north of the present latitudinal center of the species. Balsam fir and black spruce are the only exceptions. Some of the greatest advances have been registered by tree species that we normally associate with warmer valleys or the more southern fringes of our region, such as basswood and northern red oak. We have evidence, too, that on mountain slopes hardwoods are slowly encroaching upon the lower edge of the spruce-fir zone. Together these observations seem to strengthen predictions that the spruce-fir forest type may eventually be confined to smaller, higher, and more isolated mountain tops, or pushed out of the region altogether, and that northern hardwoods may be invaded or possibly replaced by oak-hickory or oak-pine forest communities currently scattered throughout drier areas of southern Maine, southern New Hampshire and Vermont, and western Massachusetts.

While it could be argued that such replacement will take a long time, given the longevity of our dominant tree species, remember that periodic disturbance is a prevalent factor in the shaping of the northern forest, and that once other tree species establish seedlings in the forest understory, change in community composition can occur quickly following loss of the overstory dominants from insects, disease, wind throw, or fire. As a case in point, central New England is already seeing extensive death and replacement of eastern hemlock as an invasive insect pest, the hemlock woolly adelgid, is pushing northward (the geographic range of this insect is limited by low winter temperatures that kill adults active during the winter, but warmer winters have allowed the insect to advance as far as southern Vermont and New Hampshire). Elimination of hemlock from the overstory of forests in Connecticut and Massachusetts has resulted in a complete shift in dominance to a mixed hardwood forest comprised mostly of black birch, red oak, and red maple. Just what the northern forest might look like following replacement of overstory dominants is difficult to say, since newcomers will migrate at different rates (depending partly on how they are disseminated) and may experience different degrees of success in establishing themselves in new territory.

As for the fate of animal species, it is quite possible that some, particularly those with short generation times, will be able to adapt to a new climatic regime. Long-term research has shown, for example, that the mosquito inhabiting the pitcher plant (see "Double-Dealing Plants" on page 62) is already responding to the delayed onset of freezing temperatures in the fall by entering hibernation a week later now than it did in the 1970s—a significant adjustment in timing that is normally regulated by day length and is critical to the insect's overwinter survival. In another example, some female red squirrels in northern locations have adjusted their breeding times by almost three weeks with the earlier arrival of spring. Those with the genetic propensity to do so (not all do) give their offspring a significant advantage at the other end of the summer, as their young are bigger and become independent sooner than their later-born cohorts. This, in turn, gives them a head start on hoarding food for winter, enhancing their survival and, hence, future reproductive potential.

Other species may simply shift their ranges northward with the changing climate and vegetation. We are already witnessing this on several different fronts. A number of bird species, for example, now appear at far higher latitudes during winter than was the case in the late 1960s when coordinated efforts to monitor winter populations began. This is particularly true of species that regularly make use of supplemental food at bird feeders, but a large number of woodland species that rarely visit feeders have also pushed their ranges northward. The purple finch, a widespread species that breeds in the northern conifer forests and winters as far south as the Gulf states, has extended its range more than 400 miles northward during the past 40 years, even while its numbers seem to be in decline (see Figure 30). Though this species is a frequent visitor to bird feeders, it is not likely that supplemental food alone explains this extraordinary expansion. More telling, perhaps, is that in years of irruptions—periodic and dramatic invasions of lower latitudes when failure of seed crops forces birds out of the North—the purple finch no longer retreats as far south as it once did. Two other birds closely associated with the northern forest, the boreal chickadee and spruce grouse, have also expanded their range limits northward by almost 300 miles (see Figures 31 and 32). It seems reasonable to expect similar shifts in the future by white-winged and red crossbills, three-toed and black-backed woodpeckers, and the gray jay—birds whose ranges are currently centered in the boreal forests of Canada and which, in the Northeast, are at the southern edge of their geographic distribution. While some of these birds will likely disappear from the northern forest as our climate warms further, there are others of more southern affinity—the brown-headed nuthatch and loggerhead shrike to name two—that seem poised to move into the area.

Clearly, having room to move is a crucial element in the ability of species to keep pace with shifting climate and vegetation, and this is where, for nonflying animals, natural corridors connecting suitable habitat become critical. We have already seen how mammals of deep forest habitat, like the lynx and marten, can become "trapped" in isolated habitat patches by barriers such as expansive open land, across which they are reluctant to travel. But even with suitable corridors for dispersal, some projections suggest that climate change may occur faster than normal plant and animal migration rates can keep up with—changes requiring movement at rates perhaps ten times greater than those recorded after the retreat of the last ice sheet.

This would pose a particular problem for many animal species—reptiles, amphibians, and small mammals especially—that face numerous barriers to migration. And it would present an especially difficult situation for plants and animals of specialized habitats, such as the many bog and alpine species that may simply have no place to go. In a sense, these species too, are trapped by a wilderness of inhospitable territory around them, and in the face of rapid climate change, those that are already rare would likely disappear entirely

**FIGURE 30** The purple finch is a bird of coniferous and mixed forests, eating seeds and tree buds in winter, adding insects in spring and fruits in summer. The species is presently undergoing a significant range extension northward, but is declining in numbers in the Northeast due to competition from house finches.

**FIGURE 31** The boreal chickadee lives entirely within the coniferous forests of Canada and the northeastern United States. Already expanding its range northward, it is very likely to disappear from areas south of the Canadian border as climate continues to warm and spruce-fir zones shift northward.

**FIGURE 32** Restricted to the boreal forests of Canada and the northeastern United States, the spruce grouse is extending its range northward. Its population in the Adirondack region is currently estimated at less than 300 and it is now listed as endangered in both New York State and Vermont.

from our landscape. The northern bog lemming, for example, confined to a few mid-elevation sites in northern Maine and New Hampshire (see page 67), would almost certainly disappear from these fringe areas of the species' range, should their habitat dry up as projected. The migratory Bicknell's thrush, intimately tied to our isolated subalpine forests (see page 97), is in danger of extirpation from smaller islands of suitable breeding territory in the Catskills, Adirondacks, and Green Mountains. Breeding populations historically recorded on Mount Greylock in western Massachusetts have not been seen since the 1970s. A further increase in summer temperature of just 2 degrees is expected to reduce habitat for this bird by one-half—a loss that could push the population as a whole to dangerously low numbers. It is impossible to say at present, however, whether Bicknell's thrush has the capacity to adapt its breeding behavior and move into lower spruce-fir woodlands north of our region. A small segment of the population currently breeds in lower elevation conifer forests of the Gaspé and Saguenay River areas of Quebec.

While these examples serve to highlight some of the more dramatic responses to a warming climate, there are many more subtle and immediate consequences related to changes in our winter snow cover. Snowfall in the Northeast has declined significantly since the early 1970s, with some weather stations in the Adirondacks reporting decreases in annual totals of 40 to 60 inches. Throughout much of Vermont, New Hampshire, and Maine, total annual snowfall has decreased by 20 to 40 inches in that time. This represents a decline of about 30 percent for the region as a whole. Accompanying the decrease in depth has been an increase in average snow density, since temperatures are warmer and more precipitation is falling as rain. The decrease in total snow depth has also translated into a significant decrease in the number of days with snow on the ground.

These changes have important implications for animals that depend on the protective cover of snow for their overwinter survival (recall our discussion on page 147), especially for reptiles and amphibians that have no capacity to alter their immediate surroundings or to regulate their body temperature. Among amphibians, only the spring peeper, wood frog, and gray treefrog, all of which hibernate on land during winter, are known to survive ice formation in their body tissues. But their tolerance is limited and exposure to temperatures below 20 degrees is usually fatal. Other land-hibernating amphibians have no freezing tolerance and therefore must find places to hibernate where temperatures will not go below 32 degrees F. Because all of these animals overwinter with little more protection than that afforded by shallow soil and leaf litter, the dependable presence of snow cover—snow of sufficient depth and low-enough density to provide adequate insulation—becomes crucial. The same is true for the Northeast's reptiles. Painted turtle hatchlings are known to survive some tissue freezing, and there is anecdotal evidence suggesting that garter snakes may have the same ability, but for these and other reptiles, an insulating layer of snow can be critical. So the paradox of a warming climate is that milder winters in the Northeast, with less snow cover, may be the death of some animals that have little or no tolerance for the cold.

It seems appropriate at this point to ask if we might be overstating the potential for change based on our current understanding of climate dynamics and biotic response to warming temperatures. Interactions between the atmosphere, oceans, and land surface that drive our climate are indeed complex, and in our present state of knowledge there is still room for surprise. Yet there is much we can be reasonably certain about, especially with regard to the self-reinforcing nature of some of the global changes we are already witnessing. While we have focused so far primarily on the northern forest, some of the most important climate changes are taking place farther afield. Most significant, perhaps, is a global decline in the amount of ice and snow covering the northern hemisphere. The loss of snow cover on this scale means that less sunlight is being reflected back to space and more energy is being absorbed by the exposed land surface. Increased absorption of solar radiation, of course, further warms the earth's surface, which in turn warms the air in contact with the surface, which melts more snow and ice. Warmer surface temperatures also mean more heat is radiated back to space, but the increased $CO_2$ levels in our atmosphere are trapping much of this energy. And in polar regions where warming is most pronounced, scientists have uncovered yet another problem. We are beginning to witness a widespread thawing of permafrost—soil that has been frozen for centuries. And with this thawing, a significant amount of $CO_2$ is being released from renewed microbial activity and the breakdown of a vast pool of carbon-rich organic matter.

So it appears that upward trending temperatures will continue for a while, at least until atmospheric $CO_2$ concentrations level off again and the rate of snowmelt and permafrost thawing reaches a new equilibrium with climate. While it seems certain that climate and vegetation zones will shift in the meantime (predictions suggest northward movement of 100 to 300 miles over the next century), it is difficult to say just which species associations might characterize the northern forest in the future. The present relationship between species distribution and climate may be complicated by secondary factors—changes, for example, in disease virulence, in insect fecundity and generation times, and in host susceptibility to insects and pathogens. Climate change can also affect the natural predators and diseases of insect pests in uncertain ways, making it difficult to predict the outcome, either positive or negative, of these complex interactions.

Under any scenario, continued change in the direction that we are currently witnessing will result in some species becoming clear winners, and others certain losers. There is considerable concern, perhaps justified, that warming in our region will favor weedy, more aggressive species, including exotics, and that some of the more sedentary species, particularly those that evolved in special habitats, will disappear. But weedy species play a pioneering role in every ecosystem, and our understanding of the process of succession gives us reason to believe that in time, these early invaders will be replaced by more stable (albeit perhaps more southern) elements of the Appalachian forests. Succession may look different in detail, but it will likely work the same; it is just not clear yet who the principal players of the future will be.

# Glossary

**abscission:** Normal shedding of leaves following structural and chemical changes in a specialized tissue (the abscission layer) at the leaf base.

**adventitious roots:** Roots that develop from branches in contact with the ground.

**anthocyanins:** One of a large class of plant pigments known as flavonoids that color flower petals and fruits red or purple to attract pollinators and seed dispersers. Anthocyanins also serve to protect leaves from harmful ultraviolet radiation.

**arboreal:** Living in trees.

**balds:** Mountain summits or crests covered by grasses or thick shrub vegetation rather than forest.

**boreal:** Pertaining to the north, especially the extensive coniferous forests of northern New England, Canada, and Alaska; exhibiting northern character.

**bottom lands:** Low-lying land near water.

**brown adipose tissue:** A fatty tissue characterized by a yellow to light-brown color, having a high concentration of mitochondria and hence capable of high oxidation rates and heat production.

**caecum:** A long, tubular sac branching off from the lower intestine, serving as a fermentation chamber in non-ruminant herbivores such as the spruce grouse.

**carrion:** Dead and decaying animal matter.

**climax community:** A community of plants and animals which, through the process of succession, has reached a relatively stable, self-reproducing state.

**compound leaf:** A leaf that is subdivided into separate leaflets, often five, seven, or nine, with each attached to the main stalk of the leaf. The entire leaf, with all its leaflets, emerges from one bud in the spring and is shed as a single leaf in autumn.

**corm:** A swollen, bulb-like underground plant stem that serves as a carbohydrate storage organ.

**crop:** An enlarged part of a bird's esophagus used to store food temporarily.

**deciduous:** Shedding leaves annually.

**epidermal cells:** The outermost layer of cells on the upper and lower surfaces of a leaf.

**extirpation:** Local extinction.

**felsenmeer:** A surface of broken, angular rock fragments resulting from intense freeze-thaw activity, found in periglacial environments. Also known as a block field.

**hardwoods:** Broadleaf trees that characteristically (but not always) produce a denser wood than coniferous trees.

**heath:** Any shrub in the *Heather* or *Ericaceae* family, including blueberries, cranberries, azaleas, and rhododendrons, common on acidic soils. Heath bogs and heath balds are plant communities dominated by several members of this family.

**herbaceous:** Lacking permanent, woody stems.

**kettle hole:** A large depression created when a stranded and buried block of glacial ice melts, causing a collapse of overlying sediments.

**keystone species:** A plant or animal critical to the structure or function of a community; a species whose importance in a community is greater than might be expected on the basis of its size or abundance alone.

**krummholz:** The twisted, gnarled, and sometimes matted growth form of trees at treeline.

**lenticels:** Raised pores, usually appearing as corky, horizontal lines on the stems of woody plants, that allow the interchange of gas between the atmosphere and the interior tissue.

**mast:** The large seeds or nuts produced by certain tree species, such as beech and oak.

**mesophyll:** Plant tissue sandwiched between the upper and lower epidermis, literally meaning "middle of the leaf."

**microclimate:** Climate near the ground as modified by local topography, plants, or other objects; the immediate environment in which a plant or animal operates.

**middens:** Refuse heaps created by the repeated shucking of cone scales in one place.

**niche:** An organism's functional role or "occupation" in an ecosystem (in contrast to "habitat," which is equivalent to an organism's "address").

**overstory:** Overhead tree canopy and its environment.

**periglacial:** An environment in which the dominant geological processes are controlled by the freezing of water; near glacial in terms of climate (originally referring to areas in close proximity to glaciers).

**photosynthate:** The products of photosynthesis, especially sugars.

**pioneer:** An organism adapted to colonizing vacant or disturbed sites that are often too harsh or lacking in sufficient resources for others.

**radiational cooling:** Cooling of the earth's surface and the air near the surface, occurring chiefly at night; the propagation of energy through space.

**respiration:** In plants, the collective processes of cellular maintenance and growth utilizing the products of photosynthesis.

**riparian:** Situated along a stream or near water.

**ruminant:** An animal possessing a rumen (a compartment before the stomach), specialized for the microbial breakdown of cellulose.

**saprophytic:** Pertaining to any organism that obtains its energy from dead plant matter.

**scarify:** To break up or loosen the surface of soil; to scratch, abrade, or soften the outer coat of a seed to hasten water absorption or germination.

**second-growth forest:** A forest that has regrown after a major disturbance such as fire, insect infestation, timber harvest, or wind throw, often differing in structure or composition from the original.

**sedge:** Grass-like plants, but differing from true grasses in having solid, angular stems, usually triangular in cross-section. Typical of wet soils, often growing in tufts and spreading by rhizomes; any plant in the family *Cyperaceae*.

**senesce:** To reach later maturity; grow old.

**softwoods:** Coniferous or needle-leaved trees (term derived from the nature of conifer wood, which is generally less dense than that of broadleaf trees).

**solifluction:** The slow, downhill movement of soil or other material over an impermeable layer, typically in areas where frozen ground is thawing and saturated with water.

**spathe:** A large bract or modified leaf that forms a sheath to protect a flower.

**stylet:** A small, needle-like appendage of insects for withdrawing plant fluids.

**succession:** Continuous process of colonization, extinction, and replacement of species populations at a particular site, due either to environmental changes or to the intrinsic properties of the plants and animals.

**treeline:** The northern or elevational limit of forest growth.

**tundra:** Treeless vegetation growing beyond the forest edge, dominated by mosses, lichens, herbaceous perennials, and low-growing shrubs.

**understory:** Environment and vegetation beneath a tree canopy, typically including tree saplings or seedlings, shrubs, and ground vegetation.

**wind throw:** Trees uprooted or broken by wind.

# Index

## A

*Abies balsamea. See* balsam fir
*Acer pensylvanicum. See* striped maple
*Acer rubrum. See* red maple
*Acer saccharum. See* sugar maple
*Aegolius acadicus. See* northern saw-whet
    owl
agriculture, 10
*Alces alces. See* moose
alpine bilberry, 64
alpine zone, 110–129
    characteristics of, 110–113
    geology of, 124–129
    lichen in, 120
    plants of, 113–115, 121–124
    wildflowers of, 116–119
American beaver, 10, 50
    hoarding behavior of, 141–142
    in winter, 143–144
American beech, 17, 68–72, 74
    beech bark disease and, 73
American marten, 50
    winter tracks of, 148
American mountain ash, 76
American redstart, 89
American toad, 137, 138
amphibians, 137–139
    climate change and, 160
Appalachian Trail, 102
arethusa, 40
*Arethusa bulbosa. See* arethusa
*Arisaema triphyllum. See* Jack-in-the-
    pulpit
*Armillaria bulbosa,* 136
aspen. *See* quaking aspen
autumn, 131–137, 140–142
avalanches, 98

## B

balsam fir, 28, 30, 33, 69, 94
    climate change and, 156
    forest succession and, 10, 17

moose and, 44
    in subalpine forests, 108–109
balsam poplar, 17, 30
barren ground caribou, 1
*Basidiomycetes* (fungus), 137
basswood, 156
Baxter State Park, 22–23
bay-breasted warbler, 47
beavers. *See* American beaver
beech bark disease, 73
beech trees. *See* American beech
Berkshire Hills, xii
*Betula alleghaniensis. See* yellow birch
*Betula papyrifera. See* paper birch
*Betula populifolia. See* gray birch
Bicknell, Eugene, 97
Bicknell's thrush, 96–98
    climate change and, 159–160
bigtooth aspen, 17
birch trees. *See* gray birch; paper birch;
    yellow birch
birds
    in autumn, 137, 140
    climate change and, 158–159
    of coniferous forests, 52–55
    of hardwood forests, 89–90, 91
    of subalpine forests, 96–98
    *. See also* individual species
black-and-white warbler, 92
black-backed woodpecker, 47
    climate change and, 158
black bear, 9, 51
black birch, 157
blackburnian warbler, 46, 54
black cherry, 17, 69, 81
black chokeberry, 29
black crowberry, 64
blackpoll warbler, 46, 54, 96
black spruce, 1, 17, 28–30, 34, 63
    climate change and, 156
    in subalpine forests, 107–108
black-throated green warbler, 46, 54

block streams, 125–126
bloodroot, 86
blueberry, 29
bog laurel, 66
bog rosemary, 66
bog succession, 64–67
*Bonasa umbelluss. See* ruffed grouse
boreal chickadee, 47
    climate change and, 158–159
broomsticking, 106
brown fat, 137, 144, 151, 163
brown-headed nuthatch, 158
buckbean, 58
*Bufo americanus. See* American toad
bunchberry, 29, 39, 95

**C**
Canada lynx, 44, 46, 51
Canada mayflower, 29, 38, 95
Cape May warbler, 47, 68
*Carduelis pinus. See* pine siskin
*Castor canadensis. See* American beaver
*Catharsus guttatus. See* hermit thrush
cattails, 57
Chittenden, Alfred, 11
*Clethrionomys gapperi. See* southern red-
   backed vole
climate, 3–7
    treeline and, 104–110
    . *See also* climate change
climate change, 153–162
    birds and, 157–159
    effect of on northern forests,
      156–162
    measurement of, 153–154
    warming associated with, 154–155
climax communities, 14, 17, 41, 72, 163
clintonia, 29, 39, 94, 95
*Clintonia borealis. See* clintonia
cloudberry, 64
cloud cover, 5–6, 111
coniferous forests, 28–56
    birds of, 46–47, 52–56
    characteristics of, 28–30
    climate and, 7
    climate change and, 153, 156
    disturbance in, 41
    evergreen advantage of, 42
    forest succession and, 14–16

mammal species, 43–44, 46, 48–52
natural history of, 1–2
spruce budworm and, 45
tree species, 31–37
wildflower species, 38–40
*Contopus virens. See* eastern wood pewee
*Coptis trifolia. See* goldthread
*Cornus canadensis. See* bunchberry
coydog, 21
coyotes, 21–22
    winter tracks of, 149
creeping snowberry, 29, 38
*Crepidotus applanatus,* 134
*Cypripedium acaule. See* pink lady's slipper

**D**
deer. *See* white-tailed deer
deer mouse, 48, 96, 140
    forest succession and, 16
deer's hair sedge, 65
*Dendroica coronata. See* yellow-rumped
   warbler
*Dendroica fusca. See* blackburnian warbler
*Dendroica striata. See* blackpoll warbler
*Dendroica virens. See* black-throated green
   warbler
*Desmognathus fuscus. See* northern dusky
   salamander
diapensia, 111
*Dicentra culcullaria. See* Dutchman's
   breeches
dieback zones, 98–102
disturbance
    in subalpine forests, 98–102
downslope creep, 127–128
*Drepanocladus fluitans,* 64–65
dusky salamander, 137
Dutchman's breeches, 86
dwarf willow, 110

**E**
eastern chipmunk, 91
eastern cottontail, 91
eastern hemlock, 31, 69, 72
    climate change and, 157
    forest succession and, 17
    in old-growth forests, 8
eastern white pine, 32, 69, 72
    forest succession and, 10–11, 14, 17

in old-growth forests, 8
eastern wood pewee, 90, 92
*Erethizon dorsatum. See* North American
porcupine
*Erythronium americanum. See* trout lilly
evening grosbeak, 47, 92
evergreen advantage, 42
exotic species, 162

**F**

*Fagus grandifolia. See* American beech
fall colors, 133
felsenmeer, 94, 124–125, 164
fire cherry. *See* pin cherry
fir trees. *See* balsam fir
fir waves, 99–102
floristic relay succession, 13–14
flying squirrels, 43, 72, 91, 140
forest succession and, 16–17
foamflower, 86
forest succession, 10–11, 13–18, 69–72
climate change and, 156–158
foxes. *See* gray fox; red fox
*Fraxinus americana. See* white ash
frogs. *See* gray tree frog; spring peeper;
wood frog
frost wedging, 124
fungi, 132–137
forest succession and, 16

**G**

*Ganoderma tsugae,* 134
garter snakes, 161
*Gaultheria hispidula. See* creeping
snowberry
golden-crowned kinglet, 46, 55
goldthread, 29, 38, 95
goosefoot maple. *See* striped maple
gray birch, 14, 17, 83
gray fox, 91, 141
gray jay, 47, 53
climate change and, 158
gray treefrog, 137, 160
Greylock, Mount, xii
ground-foraging ovenbird, 91

**H**

haircap moss, 95
hardwood forests, 68–93
beech bark disease in, 73
birds of, 89–92
characteristics of, 68–70, 92–93
climate and, 7
climate change and, 153, 156
forest succession and, 11, 69–72
mammals in, 72, 91
natural history of, 2–3
old-growth, 8
trees of, 74–85
wildflowers of, 86–88
wild turkey and, 24–25
heath bogs, 56–68
hemlock trees. *See* eastern hemlock
hemlock wooly adelgid, 157
*Hepatica nobilis. See* round-lobed hepatica
hermit thrush, 89, 91
hoarding, 140–142
hobblebush, 30, 88, 94
human history, 7–13
eradication of carnivores, 18–20
*Hygrophoropsis aurantiaca,* 134
*Hylochichla mustelina. See* wood thrush

**I**

insectivorous plants, 62–63
Isle Royale, 44

**J**

Jack-in-the-pulpit, 87
jumping mice
forest succession and, 16

**K**

Keeling, C. David, 153–154

**L**

Labrador tea, 29, 66
landslides, 98
*Larix laricina. See* Tamarack
leaf abscission, 131–133, 163
least flycatchers, 91
leatherleaf, 58–60, 66

*Lepus americanus. See* showshoe hare
lichens, 29, 120
    forest succession and, 16
*Linnaea borealis. See* twinflower
loggerhead shrike, 158
logging, 8–12, 70, 104
*Loxia leucoptera. See* white-winged
    crossbill
lynx. *See* Canada lynx
*Lynx canadensi. See* Canada lynx

## M

Mahoosuc Range, 64–65
*Maianthemum canadense. See* Canada
    mayflower
mammals
    in autumn, 140–142
    of coniferous forests, 48–52
    of hardwood forests, 72, 91
    of subalpine forests, 96
    . *See also* individual species
maple trees. *See* red maple; striped
    maple; sugar maple
Maritime Provinces, xiii
marshes, 56–59
martens, 43–44
*Martes americana. See* American marten
Mauna Loa Observatory, 153–154
meadow vole, 16
microbial succession, 132–137
miniaturization, 110–111
mink, 43
Monadnock, Mount, xii
moose, 44, 51
    in winter, 145–147
mosses, 16
    . *See also* sphagnum moss
mountain ash, 30, 93
mountain effect, 5–6
mountain holly, 29
mountain lions, 9, 18–21
mountain maple, 30
mountain serviceberry, 30
musk oxen, 1
*Mustela erminea. See* short-tailed weasel
mycorrhizal relations, 136

## N

Native Americans, 7–8
natural history, 1–3
needle ice, 125–128
North American porcupine, 50, 72, 96
    winter tracks of, 149
northern bog lemming, 67–68
    climate change and, 159
northern dusky salamander, 139
Northern Forest Alliance, xiii
Northern Forest conservation initiative,
    xiii
northern forests
    alpine zone, 110–129
    amphibians of, 138–139
    animal populations, 18–25
    autumn in, 131–135
    birds of, 52–55, 89–90, 159
    climate, 3–7
    coniferous woodlands, 28–56
    definition of, xiii
    effect of climate change on, 153–176
    fungi of, 134–137
    hardwood forests, 68–93
    heath bogs, 56–68
    human history, 7–13
    mammals of, 48–51
    natural history, 1–3
    plant succession, 13–18
    subalpine forests, 93–110
    treeline in, 102–110
    wildflowers of, 38–40, 86–88,
        116–119
    winter in, 143–152
    winter tracks in, 148–149
northern hardwood association, 68–69
northern parula, 46
northern raven, 47
northern saw-whet owl, 55
northern water shrew, 42
*Notophthalmus viridescens. See* red-
    spotted newt

## O

oak trees, 156–157
old-growth forests, 8, 22
old man's beard, 29

Olympic Peninsula, 6
Ouellet, Henri, 97
*Oxalis montana. See* wood sorrel

**P**

painted turtle, 137, 160
palm warbler, 68
paper birch, 30, 69, 71, 72, 84
    forest succession and, 14, 17
    in subalpine forests, 93, 95
parasitic fungi, 16
*Paxillus atrotomentosus,* 134
periglacial landforms, 124, 165
*Perisoreus canadensis. See* gray jay
*Peromyscus maniculatus. See* deer mouse
*Picea mariana. See* black spruce
*Picea rubens. See* red spruce
pin cherry, 69, 71–72, 80
    forest succession and, 14, 17
pine grosbeak, 47, 52
pine siskin, 47, 52, 92
pine trees. *See* eastern white pine
*Pinicola enucleator. See* pine grosbeak
pink lady's slipper, 88
*Pinus strobus. See* Eastern white pine
pioneer species, 14–15, 17, 165
pitcher plant, 59, 62–63
    climate change and, 157
plant communities. *See* alpine ares;
    coniferous forests; hardwood forests;
    heath bogs; subalpine forests
plant succession, 13–18
    . *See also* forest succession
*Plethodon cinereus. See* red-backed
    salamander
*Populus tremuloides. See* quaking aspen
porcupines. *See* North American
    porcupine
predator-prey interactions, 44
predators, 18–21, 44
*Prunus pensylvanica. See* pin cherry
*Prunus serotina. See* black cherry
*Pseudacris crucifer. See* spring peeper
purple finch, 157–159
pygmy shrew, 144

**Q**

quaking aspen, 25, 82
    forest succession and, 14, 17
    in subalpine forests, 95
quaking bogs, 58
Quebec, xiii

**R**

railroads, 8–9
*Rana sylvatica. See* wood frog
red-backed salamander, 139
red-breasted nuthatch, 47, 52
red crossbill, 47
red fox, 72
red maple, 72, 77
    climate change and, 157
    forest succession and, 17
red oak, 156–157
redpolls, 92
red-spotted newt, 137, 139
red spruce, 6, 30, 35, 69, 72
    forest succession and, 10, 15, 17
    in subalpine forests, 93
red squirrel, 43, 49
    climate change and, 157
    hoarding behavior of, 141–142
    in winter, 143–144
    winter tracks of, 149
red trillium, 87
*Regulus satrapa. See* golden-crowned
    kinglet
reptiles, 160–161
rime ice, 100–101, 109
river otters, 43
round-leaved sundew, 64
round-lobed hepatica, 87
ruffed grouse, 25, 89, 91
Russell, Howard S., 7–8

**S**

*Sanguinaria canadensis. See* bloodroot
saprophytic fungi, 16, 135–136, 165
scatter hoarding, 140
Schaechter, Moselio, 136
*Setophaga ruticilla. See* American redstart
sheep laurel, 29, 63, 66

short-tailed shrew, 16
short-tailed weasel, 49, 144–145
    winter tracks of, 148
*Sitta canadensis. See* red-breasted
    nuthatch
*Sitta carolinensis. See* white-breasted
    nuthatch
small bog cranberry, 64
snow cover, 147, 150–151
    climate change and, 154, 160
snowshoe hare, 44, 46, 49, 96
    winter tracks of, 148
solifluction, 127–128, 166
*Sorbus americana. See* American
    mountain ash
*Sorex palustris. See* water shrew
sorted circles, 127
southern red-backed vole, 48, 72, 96, 140
*Sphagnum fuscum,* 67
sphagnum moss, 56–57, 59–62, 64–65,
    67–68, 95
spinulose wood fern, 95
spring beauty, 69
spring peeper, 137, 138, 160
spruce budworm, 45, 47
spruce-fir woodlands. *See* coniferous
    forests; subalpine forests
spruce grouse, 47, 56
    climate change and, 158–159
spruce trees. *See* black spruce; red spruce;
    white spruce
squirrels. *See* red squirrel
starflower, 29, 39
storm tracks, 4
striped maple, 79
subalpine forests, 93–110
    birds of, 96–98
    characteristics of, 93–96
    climate of, 5
    disturbance in, 98–102
    limits to tree growth in, 102–110
sugar maple, 68–72, 78
    forest succession and, 17
sundew, 59, 61, 63
Swainson's thrush, 46
swamp maple. *See* red maple
sweet gale, 58

**T**
Tamarack, 28, 36, 63
    forest succession and, 17
*Tamiasciurus hudsonicus. See* red squirrel
Thompson, Zadock, 10, 19
three-toed woodpecker, 47
    climate change and, 158
*Thuja occidentalis. See* white cedar
*Tiarella cordifolia. See* foamflower
*Trametes versicolor,* 134
treeline, 102–110
trees (detailed descriptions)
    of coniferous forests, 31–37
    of hardwood forests, 74–85
*Trientalis borealis. See* starflower
*Trillium erectum. See* red trillium
trout lily, 69, 88
*Tsuga canadensis. See* Eastern hemlock
tundra. *See* alpine zone
twinflower, 29, 40

**U**
understory tolerance, 17
*Ursus americanus. See* black bear

**V**
veery, 91
*Viburnam lantanoides. See* hobblebush
voles. *See* southern red-backed vole

**W**
Washington, Mount, 98, 104, 108
    alpine regions of, 128–129
    climate of, 3, 111
water-conservation adaptations, 66
water shrew, 48
weasels. *See* short-tailed weasel
Westveld, Marinus, 11
wetlands. *See* heath bogs; marshes
white ash, 69, 75
    forest succession and, 17
white-breasted nuthatch, 90, 92
white cedar, 29, 37
    forest succession and, 10, 17
white-footed mouse, 91
White Mountains, 3, 9
white pine. *See* eastern white pine

white spruce, 30
    forest succession and, 10, 15, 17
white-tailed deer, 10, 22–23, 72
    in winter, 145–147
white-throated sparrow, 46, 55, 96
white-winged crossbill, 47, 53
    climate change and, 158
wildflowers
    of alpine zone, 116–119
    of coniferous forests, 38–40
    of hardwood forests, 86–88
wildlife, 18–25
    forest succession and, 16–17
    human eradication of, 9–10
    . *See also* amphibians; birds;
          mammals; individual species
wild raisin, 30
wild turkey, 10, 23–25, 91
wind damage, 105–107
wind throw, 41, 98–99, 156, 166
winter, 143–151
winterberry, 29
wolves, 9, 18–19, 21, 44

wood asters, 95
wood frog, 137, 138, 160
woodland caribou, 22–23
woodland jumping mouse, 91
wood sorrel, 29, 40, 94–95
wood thrush, 90, 91
woolly beech scale, 73

## X

*Xeromphalina kauffmanii,* 134

## Y

yellow birch, 68–72, 85
    forest succession and, 17
    in subalpine forests, 94
yellow-rumped warbler, 46, 53

## Z

*Zonotrichia albicollis. See* white-throated
    sparrow

# About the AMC's Efforts in the Northern Forest

The Appalachian Mountain Club (AMC) has played a leading role in the protection of the 26 million-acre Northern Forest that stretches across Maine, New Hampshire, Vermont, and New York. AMC was a founder of the Northern Forest Alliance and since 1990 has applied its conservation policy, forest ecology, and mapping expertise to inventory resources in the Northern Forest, identifying large wild land areas, shifts in ownership patterns, and priorities for conservation. This experience in Northern Forest issues led to AMC's launch of the Maine Woods Initiative, the most significant investment in land conservation in AMC's history.

AMC is a strong advocate for public land conservation funding. Initiatives such as the federal Forest Legacy Program, Maine's Land for Maine's Future program, and New Hampshire's Land Conservation and Historic Preservation program are key to protecting the Northern Forest. They rely on citizens like you letting elected officials know that land conservation is important and that these programs should be fully funded.

Through its Maine Woods Initiative, AMC has established a model for conservation that it believes can be replicated throughout the region. The Maine Woods Initiative is AMC's strategy for land conservation in Maine's 100-Mile Wilderness that addresses ecological and economic needs through a balance of outdoor recreation, resource protection, sustainable forestry, and community partnerships. To date, AMC has purchased and permanently conserved more than 66,000 acres of forestland, preserved public access for traditional uses such as hunting and fishing, renovated and upgraded three sporting camps, and begun work on a network of recreational trails and campsites that create new nature-based tourism opportunities for the region.

## Get Involved

- Speak out on regional land conservation issues by joining the Conservation Action Network at www.outdoors.org/conservation/action.
- Learn more about the Maine Woods Initiative by visiting www.outdoors.org/mwi.
- Participate in Mountain Watch. Our citizen-science program includes an alpine flower watch covering the high peaks of the Northern Forest. Visit www.outdoors.org/conservation/mountainwatch.

# ABOUT THE AUTHOR

Peter Marchand is a field biologist trained in earth sciences and systems ecology at the University of New Hampshire. He earned his doctorate investigating the physiological limits to tree growth at high elevation and then devoted much of his career to the study of forest and tundra ecosystems, traveling widely throughout North America and Europe. His research has been published in several scientific journals. Peter has shared his love of natural science with others for more than 20 years, teaching field courses for colleges and universities across the country and translating science for diverse audiences through his writing. He has contributed some 28 articles to Natural History Magazine, a publication of the American Museum of Natural History, and currently has two other books in print: *Life in the Cold* (an award-winning book now in its third edition) and *Autumn: A Season of Change,* both published by University Press of New England.

# IMAGE CREDITS

# AMC BOOK UPDATES

AMC Books strives to keep our books as up-to-date and accurate as possible. If after publishing a book we learn that trails are relocated or other information has changed, we will post the updated information online. Check for updates at www.outdoors.org/publications/books/updates.

If you find any errors in this book, please let us know by submitting them to amcbookupdates@outdoors.org or in writing to Books Editor, c/o AMC, 5 Joy Street, Boston, MA 02108. We will verify all submissions and post key updates each month. AMC Books is dedicated to being a recognized leader in outdoor publishing. Thank you for your assistance.

AMC BOOKS & MAPS

**EXPLORE THE
POSSIBILITIES**

# More Books from the Outdoor Experts

## AMC's Complete Guide to Trail Building and Maintenance, 4th edition

BY THE STAFF OF AMC'S TRAILS DEPARTMENT

Based on AMC's 130 years of experience in building and maintaining 1,700 miles of trails from Maine to Washington, D.C., this authoritative guide teaches you everything you need to know to plan, design, build, and maintain trails.

ISBN: 978-1-934028-16-2
$19.95

## Katahdin: An Historic Journey—Legends, Explorations, and Preservation of Maine's Highest Peak

BY JOHN NEFF

This book takes readers on a journey through this renowned mountain's history, legend, and legacy— from American Indian tales, to logging and trail development, to current conservation efforts.

ISBN: 978-1-929173-62-4
$19.95

## The Wildest Country: Exploring Thoreau's Maine

BY J. PARKER HUBER

This updated, full-color edition follows famed naturalist Henry David Thoreau's sojourns in Maine and offers modern commentary on how the route has changed.

ISBN: 978-1-934028-09-4
$19.95

## AMC Field Guide to the New England Alpine Summits, 2nd edition

BY NANCY SLACK AND ALLISON BELL

AMC's field guide captures the splendor of the rare, yet accessible, alpine zone of northern New England. Full-color photos and comprehensive information bring to life the fascinating ecosystem of delicate flowers, hardy plants, and remarkable wildlife of this unpredictable climate.

ISBN: 1-929173-89-X
$16.95

---

## AMC Books & Maps: Explore the Possibilities

Shop online at www.outdoors.org/amcstore or call 800-262-4455
Appalachian Mountain Club • 5 Joy Street • Boston, MA 02108